FACE READING ESSENTIALS
PALACES & POSITIONS

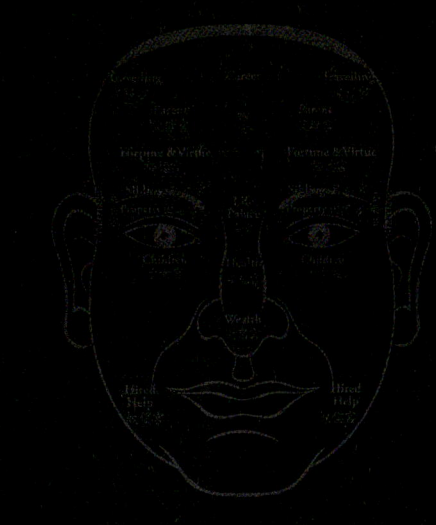

Face Reading Essentials - Palaces & positions

Copyright © 2011 by Joey Yap
All rights reserved worldwide.
First Edition July 2011
Second Print December 2012

All intellectual property rights contained or in relation to this book belongs to Joey Yap.

No part of this book may be copied, used, subsumed, or exploited in fact, field of thought or general idea, by any other authors or persons, or be stored in a retrieval system, transmitted or reproduced in any way, including but not limited to digital copying and printing in any form whatsoever worldwide without the prior agreement and written permission of the author.

The author can be reached at:

Joey Yap Research International Sdn. Bhd. (939831- H)
19-3, The Boulevard, Mid Valley City,
59200 Kuala Lumpur, Malaysia.
Tel   : +603-2284 8080
Fax   : +603-2284 1218
Website : www.masteryacademy.com

DISCLAIMER:

The author, Joey Yap and the publisher, JY Productions Sdn Bhd, have made their best efforts to produce this high quality, informative and helpful book. They have verified the technical accuracy of the information and contents of this book. Any information pertaining to the events, occurrences, dates and other details relating to the person or persons, dead or alive, and to the companies have been verified to the best of their abilities based on information obtained or extracted from various websites, newspaper clippings and other public media. However, they make no representation or warranties of any kind with regard to the contents of this book and accept no liability of any kind for any losses or damages caused or alleged to be caused directly or indirectly from using the information contained herein.

Published by JY Productions Sdn. Bhd. (944330-D)

INDEX

The 12 Palaces		17
1	Life Palace	18
2	Career Palace	20
3	Wealth Palace	22
4	Property Palace	24
5	Health Palace	26
6	Marriage Palace	28
7	Children palace	30
8	Parent Palace	32
9	Siblings Palace	34
10	Hired Help Palace	36
11	Travelling Palace	38
12	Fortune & Virtue Palace	40
The Cosmic Trinity (The Three Region)		43
13	Upper (Heaven)	46
14	Middle (Man)	48
15	Lower (Earth)	50
The Six Mansions		53
16	The Two Upper Mansions (Heavenly Storage)	56
17	The Two Middle Mansions (represented by the cheeks)	58
18	The Two Lower Mansions (represented by chin /jaw bone)	60

The Five Mountains		63
19	Mountain Tai (East)	66
20	Mountain Heng (South)	68
21	Mountain Song (Center)	70
22	Mountain Hua (West)	72
23	Mountain Heng (North)	74
The Five Officers		77
24	Eyes - Vigilance Officer	80
25	Ears - Listening Officer	82
26	Mouth - Information Officer	84
27	Nose - Chief Justice Officer	86
28	Eyebrows - Insurance Officer	88
The Four Rivers		91
29	Ears – Rivers	94
30	Eyes – Streams	96
31	Mouth – the canal	98
32	Nose – the creek	100
The Five Stars		103
33	Metal Star – Right Ear	104
34	Wood Star- Left Ear	106
35	Water Star – Mouth	108
36	Fire Star – Forehead	110
37	Earth Star – Nose	112

Six Brightness		115
38	Purple Qi (Zi Qi)	116
39	Moon Polo (Yue Bei)	118
40	Luo Hou (Rahu)	120
41	Ji Duo (Ketu)	122
42	Great Yang and Great Yin	124
The Four Academic Halls		127
43	The Officer Academic Hall - Eyes	128
44	The Prosperous Academic Hall - Forehead	130
45	The Internal Academic Hall - Teeth	132
46	The External Academic Halls - Ears	134
The Eight Academic Halls		137
47	The High Bright Academic Hall	138
48	The High Broad Academic Hall	140
49	The Big Bright Academic Hall	142
50	The Elegant Academic	144
51	The Intelligent Academic Hall	146
52	The Loyal Academic Hall	148
53	The Broad Virtuous Academic Hall	150
54	The Bamboo- shoot Level Academic Hall	152

宫位

The Essentials of Face Reading

The Face Reading Essentials series offers a crash course in the study of Mian Xiang (Chinese Art of Face Reading). Mian Xiang teaches us to 'read' the human face like a book. Face shape, structure, symmetry, face contours, features, facial expressions, Qi colours and more make up the overall picture when it comes to any given face. The raw data is there for anyone to see, Mian Xiang is simply a system which teaches anyone willing to learn to make sense of the story which each individual face tells.

There is a lot of information to process when you look at a face, and so I create the Face Reading Essentials series with the specific aim of breaking things down in a step by step manner for the layman.

The previous books in this series have been a resounding success with people keen to learn about Face Reading in a simple straightforward fashion. I have decided to expand upon the series with 5 new books, each of which is dedicated to a specific feature or aspect of Mian Xiang. My readers can now take their studies to the next level!

Mian Xiang instructs us to look either at specific points and features of the face (Fixed Position Reading 定流法) or, if we want to know more, to look at many features simultaneously and make sense of what they mean together (Combination Position Reading 混流法). Different features give us insight into different traits of the person in question. Combination Position Reading techniques give us a more in-depth analysis of a particular person but Fixed Position Reading represents an ideal starting point

for beginners. This technique is simple, easy to learn and effective, and accordingly, the Face Reading Essentials books deal with Fixed Position Reading.

Palaces and Positions

This book focuses on the Palaces and Positions of Face Reading, an understanding of which forms the essential backbone of Mian Xiang. The Twelve Palaces govern the twelve predominant aspects of a person's life.

With the Twelve Palaces, you can gain insight into a person's life, career, health, and much more. You can learn about the state of their relationships with parents and siblings, and predisposition towards travelling as well as his or her perceptions of life. The Twelve Palaces give us a quick snapshot reading of a person's fortune or luck in life. From nothing more than a fleeting evaluation you can derive a wealth of information.

Similarly, the Positions cover essential areas of the face that relate to a particular aspect or trajectory in one's life. By combining your reading of Palaces and Positions you will get a fuller picture of a person's obvious and hidden potential. For example, by evaluating the proper Palace or Position, you might learn that someone grew up in hard conditions but has the potential to thrive and enjoy prosperity in old age. Understanding the Palaces and Positions thus gives you a richer analysis that is more nuanced and provides more depth than is possible otherwise.

Face Reading and You

I've spent many years of my life researching various Face Reading methods and techniques, interpreting the classical texts of Mian Xiang and trying to extract the most important information for the modern age. The Face Reading Essentials books are meant to present this information to you in a relatively straightforward and easy-to-digest manner.

People aren't made to perfect specifications in a factory. Bear in mind that when you 'Face Read' someone, no one feature will perfectly match up to a 'type'. Sometimes people will possess several features which is why Face Reading requires you to do some insightful thinking of your own instead of trying to pigeon-hole everything mathematically. The answers you get from your Readings may not be black and white. The information presented here is categorized into types to that it may more easily be learned and understood but people don't always fall into types or categories. Face Reading is all about putting information together in creative ways, thinking about the context this information lies within and then piecing together a bigger picture. It is a good idea to study your own face in a mirror as you go along because practice really is the key to becoming an expert in Mian Xiang.

Should you wish to learn more about the intricacies of Mian Xiang study and practice, you might want to consider my *Homestudy Courses on Face Reading* (www.mianxianghomestudy.com). My earlier book, *Mian Xiang – Discover Face Reading* is a detailed, solid introduction to Mian Xiang, and my previous Face Reading Essentials series of books will also be helpful in your exploration.

Most importantly, be sure to enjoy Face Reading – because once you get a knack for 'Reading', you will find the practice pleasurable and enlightening. You will be surprised what you learn about yourself and others!

Joey Yap
July, 2011

Author's personal website	: www.joeyyap.com
Academy websites	: www.masteryacademy.com	www.baziprofiling.com
Joey Yap on Facebook	: www.facebook.com/joeyyapFB

The 12 Palaces

In Chinese Face Reading, the 12 Palaces of the face are associated with, and are known to govern, twelve particular aspects of a person's life. Knowing the 12 Palaces and what they represent is an important reference point and technique for reading a person's face.

This is a brief outline of what the 12 Palaces represent:

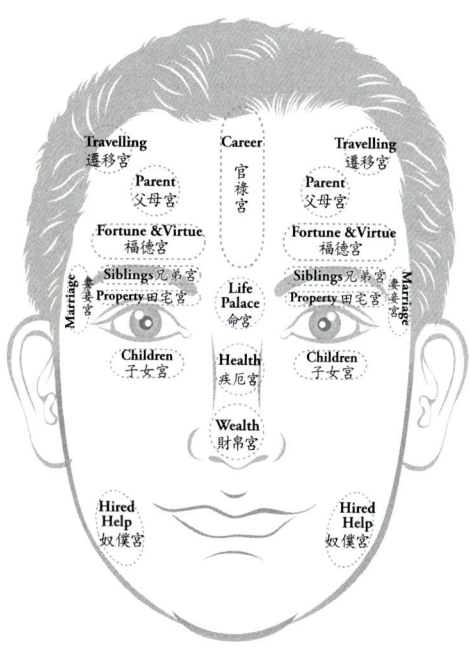

- The **Life Palace** is also known as the House of Life, and denotes the quality of a person's life in terms of wealth, intelligence, health, happiness, and prosperity.

- The **Career Palace** reveals a person's career outlook – the type of job one undertakes, as well as one's career luck and successes or failures.

- The **Wealth Palace** denotes one's aptitude with money, the propensity for wealth, and a person's luck or ability in dealing with money.

- The **Property Palace** represents a person's assets in terms of landed property, and crucially, a person's home or place of living.

- The **Health Palace** represents a person's personal health outlook, and it can also provide clues to the health of those living in the same home.

- The **Marriage Palace** represents the quality of a person's relationships, be it love, personal connection and faithfulness in relationship.

- The **Children Palace** represents a person's (potential) children, and crucially, it also denotes one's relations to one's children.

- The **Hired Help** Palace denotes all hired help in a person's life, be it professional or domestic staff.

- The **Parents Palace** denotes one's relationship with one's parents, and also the state of a parent's health. The Sun Position, as shown, indicates the father, while the Moon Position indicates the mother.

- The **Siblings Palace** denotes the quality of one's relationship with one siblings, as well as the health and wellbeing of those siblings.

- The **Travelling Palace** denotes a person's travel opportunities and outlook, and represents mobility.

- The **Fortune and Virtue** Palace denotes not so much wealth and ethics, but a person's perceptions or views on life, as well as mental and emotional happiness and fulfilment.

The 12 Palaces

Life Palace 命宮

The Life Palace is the area in between the eyebrows and the space between the eyes. The Life Palace is understood to represent the 'root of the heart'.

An ideal Life Palace is one where it's broad and big, and tall. This represents nobility. The skin and complexion around this area should be bright and smooth, indicating clarity of one's own future. If it is broad, fleshy and spacious, it denotes a person who has a positive outlook in life, is ambitious and strong-willed.

The Life Palace should ideally not have lines, as this indicates obstacles in life, and potential failure. If it appears low and sunken, then it denotes a hard-knock, chaotic life. If it's too narrow, it denotes a person who is similarly narrow-minded and conservative. If there are green or black undertones in the Life Palace area, the person is likely to endure quite a bit of dangers and disasters, whereas a red undertone signals lawsuits and inauspicious matters.

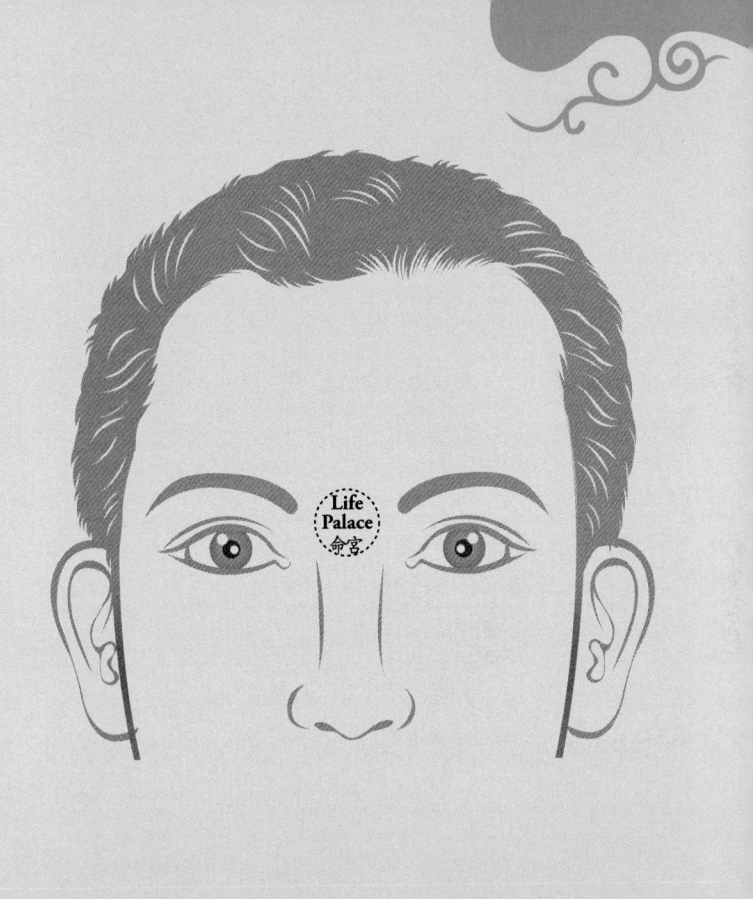

Career Palace 官祿宮

The Career Palace is located from the hairline to the Life Palace, and extends sideways until the Parents Palace. Ideally, the Career Palace should be full and fleshy and roundish in appearance, with a complexion that is bright and has clarity. A good Career Palace denotes a successful career and high social status.

If there is a bone protrusion in the Career Palace, it indicates an odd form of nobility. A straight line through the Career Palace, however, is undesirable as it signals failure and defeat. A horizontal and jagged line signals a busy and hectic life, and also the risk many potential failures in career.

If there is a blackish cast to the skin around the Career Palace, this denotes potential loss of job or career. A slanting or sunken Career Palace, meanwhile, points toward losses and failure.

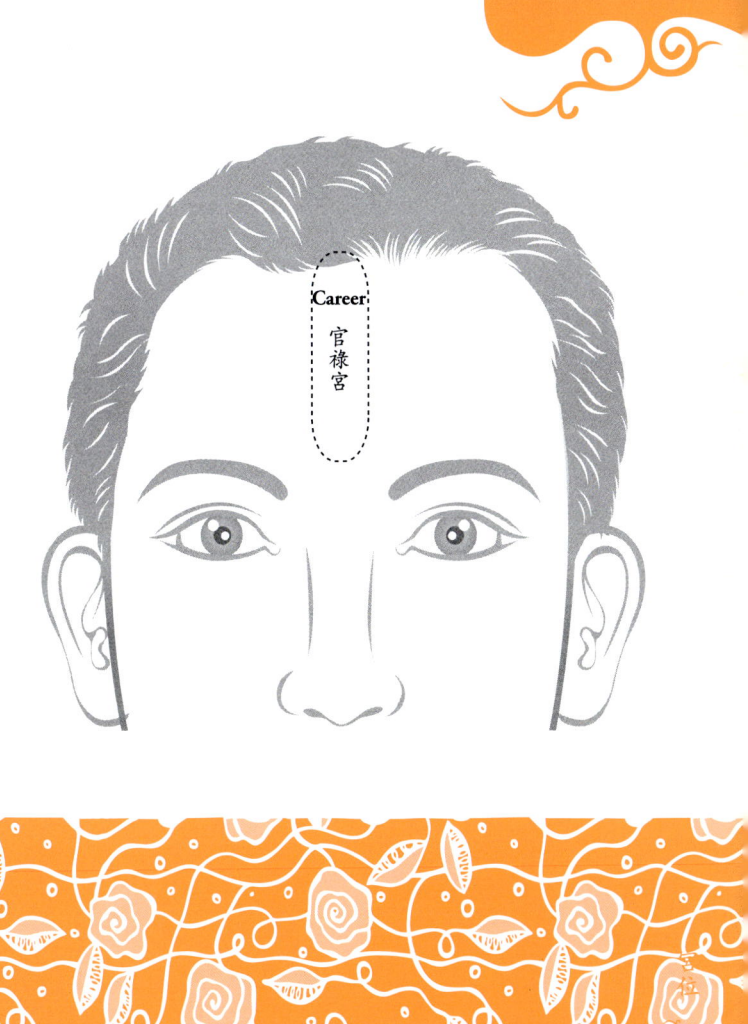

Wealth Palace 財帛宮

The Wealth Palace is located at the tip of the nose. The Wealth Palace denotes both capacity for wealth and longevity. The nose tip represents Direct Wealth (salary, direct earnings) while the Nose Wings represent Indirect Wealth (secondary income, investments, savings).

A fleshy, full Wealth Palace is a good sign as it denotes good wealth-making and wealth-retaining capacities. A tall and straight Wealth Palace also denotes reputation and nobility. If the nose tips and wings are also round, then this represents prosperity and abundance.

If the nostrils are exposed, however, then this indicates a 'flowing out' of wealth and denotes loss of wealth. This is similarly true if the skin or complexion around the Wealth Palace is darker in tone than the rest of the face. A reddish cast around the Wealth Palace indicates health problems, while a sharp and pinched nose tip denotes possible lack of wealth or even poverty. A broken or sunken Wealth Palace indicates loneliness, while a very saggy nose tip (where it almost seems to be reaching the lips) denotes a hard life with little wealth.

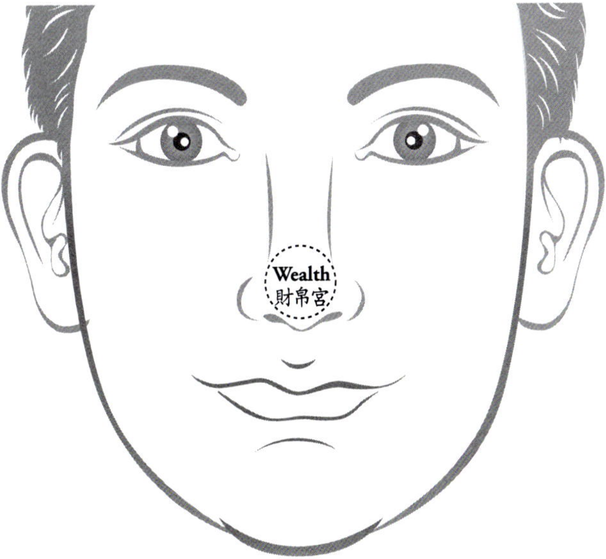

Property Palace 田宅宫

The Property Palace is the space between the eye and the eyebrow. The left Property Palace is known as Great Yang, while the right is known as Great Yin.

If the Property Palace is fleshy and broad, it denotes a big house or many properties, and a wealthy household. A sunken, not-fleshy Property Palace denotes that one has no fixed home or lacks security or stability, and is often moving around.

When reading the Property Palace, take note of the quality of the eyes, too. If the eyes are bright and shining, this indicates prosperity and the ability to own many properties. If the eyes are consistently red or bloodshot, for instance, then this indicates possible failure.

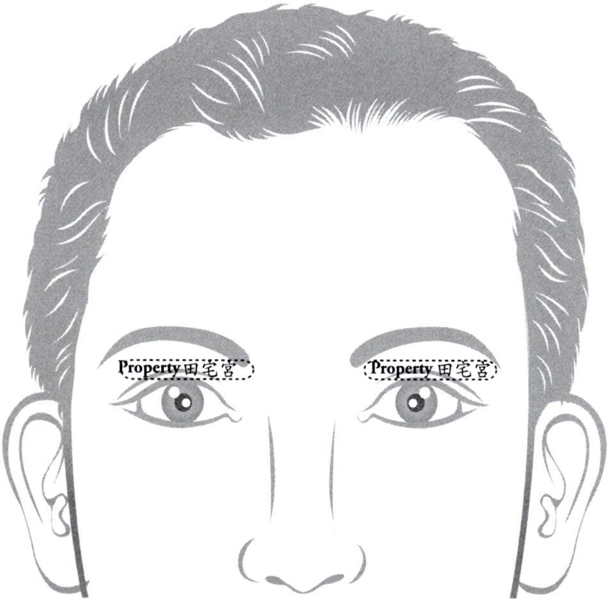

宮位

25

Health Palace 疾厄宫

The Health Palace is located at the centre of the bridge of the nose.

If it appears full and bright, it denotes good health. This is better if combined with a high Mountain Root, as this is likely to indicate robust health. A clear complexion on the Health Palace indicates a good digestive system.

However, if the Health Palace is sunken, or appears angular, then it suggests the recurrence of health problems. If the Health Palace appears bony, this denotes a bad back and poor vitality.

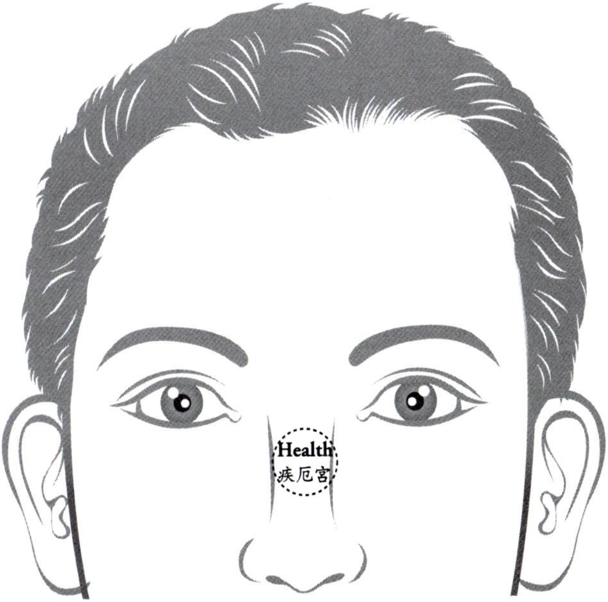

Marriage Palace 妻妾宫

The Marriage Palace for the women is the nose, whereas for men it is a finger space away from the ends of the eyes as shown in the diagram above.

For women, the Marriage Palace should ideally be full, fleshy, tall and straight – similar to all the characteristics one would want for an ideal Wealth Palace, as indicated earlier in the book.

For men, the Marriage Palace should be fleshy and clear, without blemishes or marks. If it is sunken, or if there are moles and scars, then it indicates that the wife will be domineering and controlling. A black mole here can also denote bickering or third party problem. A yellowish or greenish hue in the area also points toward ill health of the partner. Lots of lines indicate the potential for separation. If a man has Fish Tails (crinkly lines at the corner of his eyes) that reach into the Marriage Palace, it denotes Peach Blossom Lines that indicate strong sexual desires on the part of the man that can lead to extra-marital affairs.

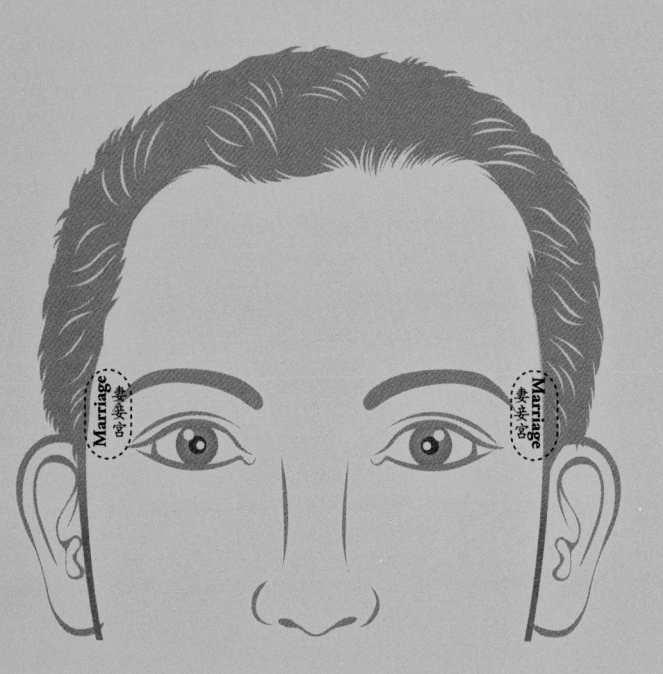

29

Children Palace
子女宮

The Children Palace is located below the eyes, or what's known as the eye-bags.

A fleshy Children Palace denotes healthy children and a good relationship with them, while a broad one can mean quite a few children! A bright, clear Children Palace also denotes that the children's lives will be successful, with a good career.

Lines in the Children Palace denote few children, while a black mole in this area suggests difficulty or poor relationship with children. A dry and sunken Children Palace may indicate illness for the children and potential disaster involving the parent-child relationship.

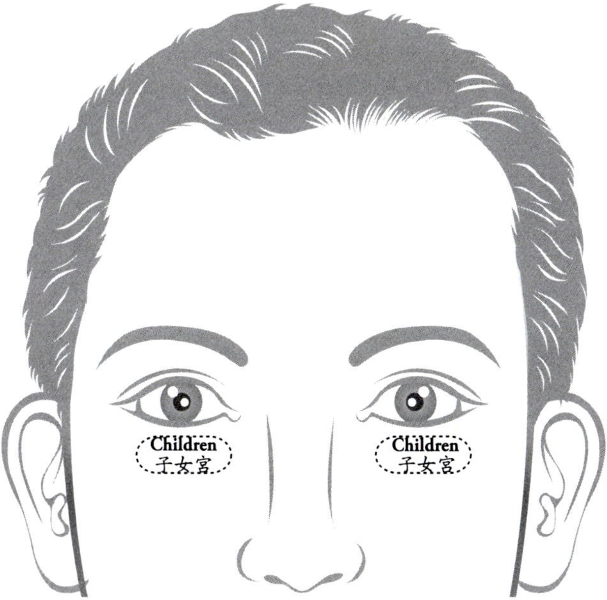
Children
子女宫
Children
子女宫

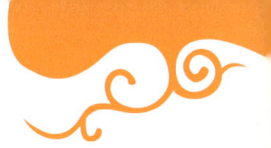

Parents Palace 父母宮

If the Parents Palace lies flat and appears full, not concave, then it denotes that a person's parents will live a long life. A fleshy and bright-toned Parents Palace means that one's parents will be well to do and have good relationship with this person.

A low, sunken Parents Palace can indicate the loss of one's father at a young age. This is also true if there are scars or protrusions here. A dented Sun position indicates a person will have a bad relationship with the father, or receive no help from the father, while a dented Moon position reveals the same about the mother.

A greenish tint or cast to the flesh at the Parents Palace suggests the risk of health problems or illness for the parents. A darkish or blackish cast to the skin indicates the loss of one's parents.

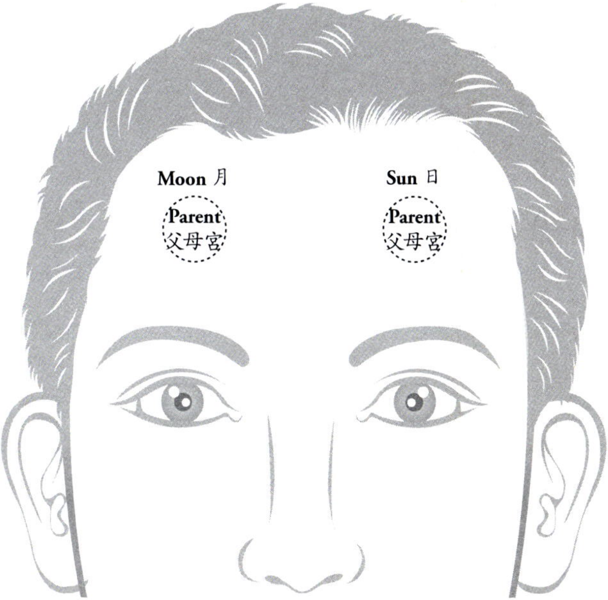

Moon 月　　　　　Sun 日
Parent　　　　　Parent
父母宮　　　　　父母宮

宮位

33

Siblings Palace 兄弟宮

The Siblings Palace is located in the region of the eyebrows and just above it. Eyebrows that are long and rise up towards the ends slightly indicate the nobility of one's siblings. If the eyebrows are clear, neat, and elegant, it means that one's siblings are likely to be helpful.

Eyebrow hair that grows in uniform direction indicates that one has a good relationship with one's siblings. A bad relationship, meanwhile, is indicated by hair that grows in opposing directions.

If the eyebrow bone protrudes towards the edge, this represents wealthy siblings – or the potential for wealth among siblings. If the eyebrow bone is broken, it denotes a difficult relationship. Short eyebrows (eyebrows shorter than the length of the eyes) represent a disharmonious relationship between the person and his or her siblings. Rough, dry-looking eyebrows indicate a person has many arguments and misunderstandings with his or her siblings over money matters.

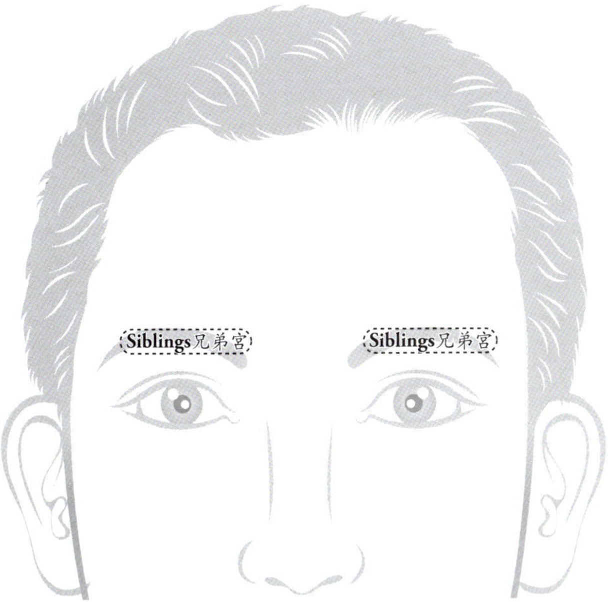

宮位

35

Hired Help Palace
奴僕宮

The Hired Help Palace is located at the bottom of the cheeks, towards the mouth on the jaw, as indicated. When reading the Hired Help Palace, it is also important to consider the quality of the chin. The chin should be broad and fleshy, in addition to taking into account the features of the Hired Help Palace itself.

A rounded, fleshy Hired Help Palace indicates a person with staff who is good in character and with a strong sense of morality. However, wrinkles at the Hired Help Palace indicate a broken structure and denotes potential problems with one's employees or domestic help.

If one's chin is small or narrow, one may be potentially stressed by one's employee as opposed to being the leader of them. A sunken area indicates that the person is liable to be betrayed by the hired help.

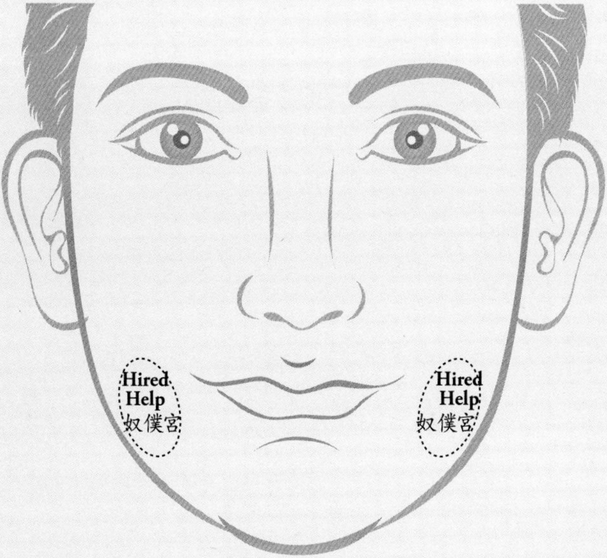

Hired Help
奴僕宮

Hired Help
奴僕宮

宮位

Travelling Palace
遷移宮

The Travelling Palace is at the left and right corners of the forehead, and it is also where one's "Sky Horse" resides. A fleshy, spacious, and broad Travelling Palace with a bright hue or clarity of complexion indicates someone who is a frequent traveller and perhaps working internationally.

A spacious Travelling Palace with a bright hue also indicates a person who is able to have multiple homes in different countries.

A sunken Travelling Palace may denote travelling that is more of a burden, in that the person will not have a fixed home or enjoy stability. If the Travelling Palace area is darker than the rest of the complexion, or has a mole, then it indicates that the person is not at all suited to travel or move about much in his or her career, and may not get the opportunity to do so.

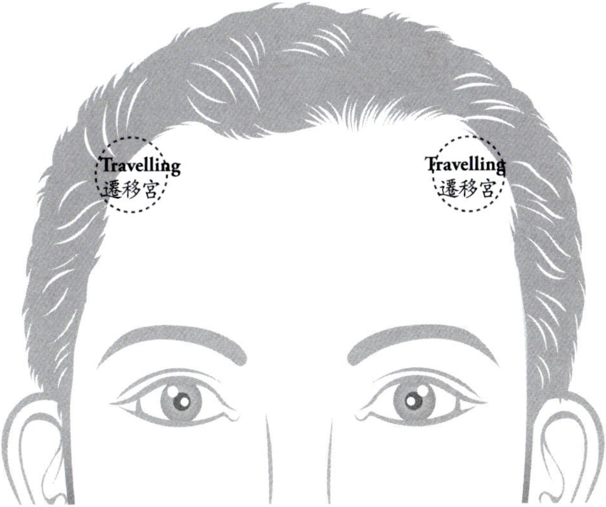

宮位

Fortune and Virtue Palace 福德宮

The Fortune and Virtue Palace is the area right above the eyebrow bone.

A strong, robust and fleshy eyebrow bone is good in that this denotes prosperity, happiness and longevity. This also indicates a strong sense of self-worth and confidence.

Eyebrow bones that are protruding noticeably and appear sharp, on the other hand, denotes an individual who can be harsh and demanding of him/herself, and who will have a challenging life because of his or her perfectionist ways.

A sunken eyebrow bone indicates a person with a cunning mentality, but one who endures a very chaotic life.

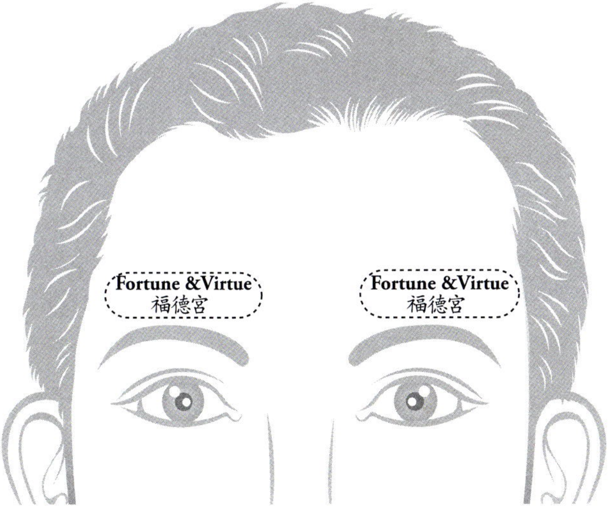

Fortune &Virtue
福德宮

Fortune &Virtue
福德宮

宮位

The Cosmic Trinity – The Three Regions

The Cosmic Trinity – The Three Regions 三停

The Three Regions of the face is directly tied to the concept of the Cosmic Trinity in Chinese Metaphysics, which is Heaven Luck, Man Luck, and Earth Luck. Heaven Luck can also be referred to as destiny, or what life has pre-ordained for a person. This refers to things that lie beyond human control – such as the family one is born to, for example.

Human Luck refers to the virtues, characteristics, and actions for each individual that potentially determines the trajectory of a person's life and how it will proceed. A person is in control of these actions and how it will affect his or her life. Finally, Earth Luck refers to the influence of the living environment (Feng Shui) to each individual's life and destiny.

Similarly, the face is also horizontally divided into three broad categories. The upper portion of the face represents Heaven, and denotes the ages 15 to 30. The middle portion represents Earth and denotes the ages 31 to 50. The lower portion represents Earth, and denotes the age 51 and upward.

An ideal face is one where all portions of the face are proportionate and symmetrical. This means that all of these factors are in balance, and no part of the face, whether Heaven, Man, or Earth, is shorter or longer, or bigger and smaller, or bonier and fleshier.

However, a perfectly-proportionate face is often a rarity – and as such, the act of Face Reading becomes all the more interesting most ordinary faces have ordinary 'flaws' that reveal a lot about a person's past, present, and future.

Upper (Heaven 天) 上停

The Upper portion or Heaven portion of the face usually runs from the hairline to the top of the Life Palace. It signifies one's luck as youth, and ideally it should be broad, with plenty of width, and fleshy. A round, broad, expansive forehead is an ideal sign.

A good Heaven portion of the face represents a person who was born to a good family with good parents, and is likely to enjoy security, education, and good family support. A good Heaven portion indicates that one's future undertakings will similarly be good.

Some consider this section of the face the most important as it is related the quality of one's life. This section governs one's innate character, one's quality of thoughts (thinking power) and his or her ability to master essential skills (education) in life. Therefore, a good Heaven portion denotes a good life.

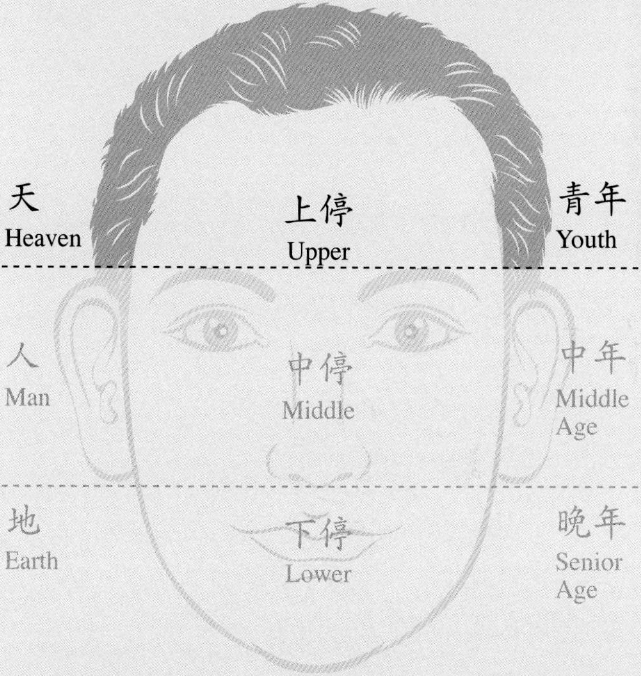

天 Heaven	上停 Upper	青年 Youth
人 Man	中停 Middle	中年 Middle Age
地 Earth	下停 Lower	晚年 Senior Age

宮位

Middle (Man 人) 中停

The middle or Man portion of the face runs from the Life Palace to the tip of one's nose.

A good Man portion of the face is fleshy and broad, but again – it's a matter of proportion to the rest of the face. A large, rounded nose, fleshy cheeks, large ears, and a full, robust appearance are key factors. This denotes good health and intelligence, and most especially, good wealth opportunities, a strong career, and an upstanding reputation amongst others.

Good, strong, prominent cheekbones represent status and authority. Unbalanced cheekbones indicate a suspicious personality, one that is always guarded, defensive, and conservative. A strong nose that is paired with firm cheeks denotes the good leadership and an influential character.

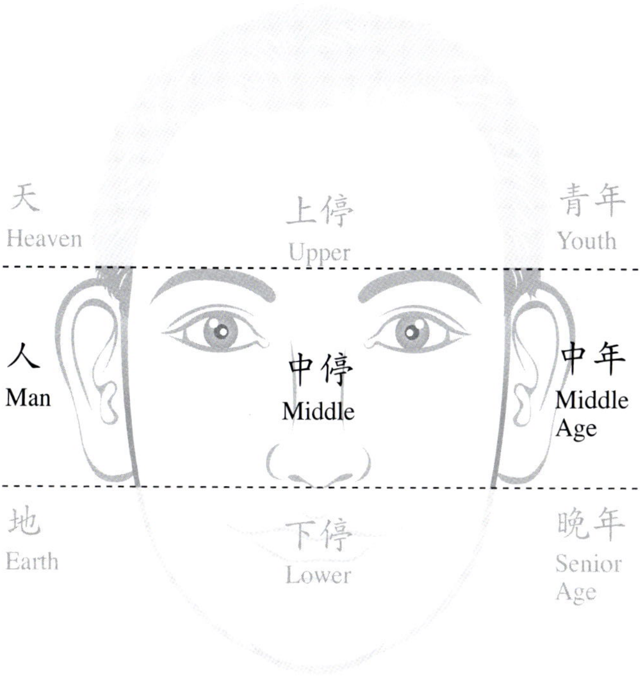

天 Heaven	上停 Upper	青年 Youth
人 Man	中停 Middle	中年 Middle Age
地 Earth	下停 Lower	晚年 Senior Age

Lower (Earth 地) 下停

The lower portion of the face, or the Earth portion, runs from the tip of the nose right to the chin. Since this represents old age, it is also important that it is fleshy and full.

It is essential to pay attention to the chin, since it represents the Earth Corner. An overly long chin is not good, as it indicates a hectic, potentially busy life that keeps one unfulfilled towards old age.

A long, pointed, and sharp or somewhat narrow Earth Corner indicates a later life that is hard and difficult, with many challenges or obstructions to be dealt with in old age.

A broad, rounded fleshy chin indicates an excellent old age - one that is filled with happiness, good health and wonderful relationships with family and friends.

天 Heaven	上停 Upper	青年 Youth
人 Man	中停 Middle	中年 Middle Age
地 Earth	下停 Lower	晚年 Senior Age

宮位

The Six Mansions

The Six Mansions 六府

The Six Mansions are located off towards the side of the face, as opposed to the central features. The Two Upper Mansions denote the Heavenly Storage on the forehead, as illustrated on Page 57. The Two Middle Mansions are represented by the cheeks. The Two Lower Mansions are represented by the area between the cheeks and the jaws, at the chin bone.

The qualifications for good Six Mansions include a full or fleshy appearance, a bright or clear skin tone, and no scars, blemishes, or defects marring any of the Six Mansions.

The Six Mansions should be understood in relation and corresponding to the Cosmic Trinity in order to assess the face. Bear in mind also that one good Mansion is the harbinger of good Wealth Luck for a ten-year period or luck cycle.

The Two Upper Mansions (Heavenly Storage) 上府

If the Upper Mansions are good, it denotes an individual who is likely to enjoy good career and wealth luck throughout his or her life.

A High Heavenly Storage is essential, meaning that the forehead and temples are broad and spacious. This means that one does not have to work excessively hard to enjoy success or wealth opportunities almost appear at the right time.

A cramped, scarred, or marked Heavenly Storage means that plenty of difficulties will plague a person throughout one's life. In particular, one will have to go through many challenges at a young age and work extremely hard, without much support of good familial connections or assistance.

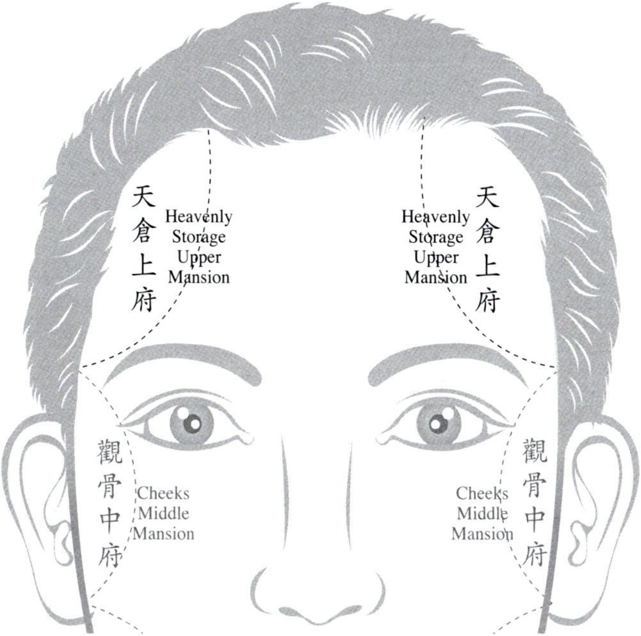

The Two Middle Mansions 中府

The Two Middle Mansions can be ascertained by the appearance of the cheeks. Robust, strong and full cheeks with prominent, steady cheekbones are all good signs.

A good Middle Mansion denotes strong wealth luck and prosperity during middle age, with the ability for the person to expand his or her business and career and secure an outstanding financial standing and reputation. As cheekbones represent status and authority, this is the stage in life where one 'makes a mark' in the world, so to speak.

A bad Middle Mansion will be broken, uneven, or sunken, or particularly narrow and cramped in relation to the rest of the face. This denotes lack of success and subsequent reputation – one may be doing many things with one life but not deriving any achievement from it, and thus suffering from the burdens of hard work without any of the fruits of one's labour.

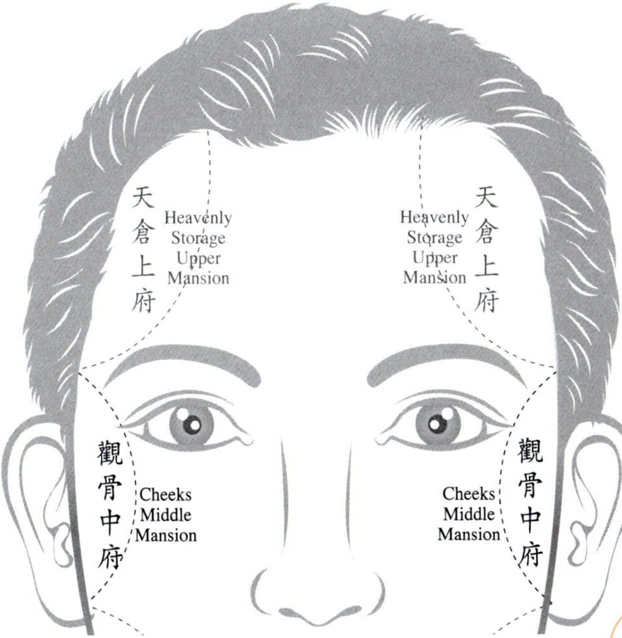

The Two Lower Mansions 下府

The Two Lower Mansions, as determined by a square-shaped Earth Corner (jawline and chin) indicate good luck and prosperity, as well as fulfilment, later on in life.

A good Lower Mansion is thus desirable because it indicates a peaceful and fulfilled old age, where one has most of one's needs met.

A weak Lower Mansion denotes not only hardships, lingering health concerns and problems in old age, but potential loneliness and isolation where one is bereft of support from loved ones and a shared community.

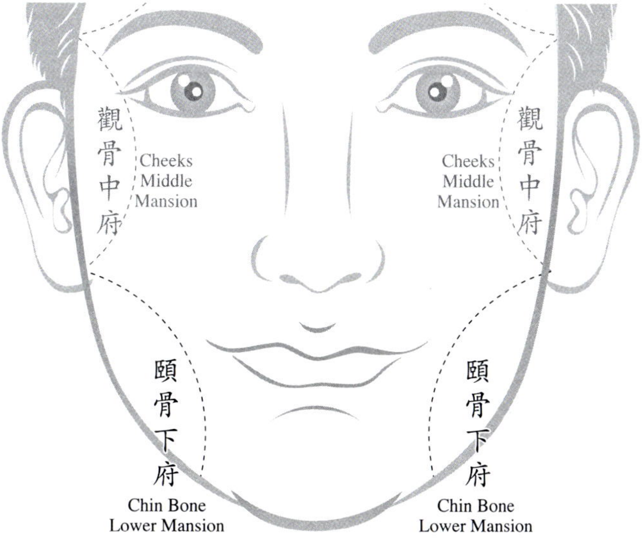
觀骨中府
Cheeks
Middle
Mansion
觀骨中府
Cheeks
Middle
Mansion
頤骨下府
Chin Bone
Lower Mansion
頤骨下府
Chin Bone
Lower Mansion

The Five Mountains

The Five Mountains
五嶽

The Five Mountains is another crucial reference point from which to do Face Reading. Essentially, when read in tandem with the Cosmic Trinity, it reveals greater clues about a person's overall propensity for success and current state of life.

The Five Mountains are divided as such:

- Mountain Tai (East) – the left cheekbone
  東嶽泰山
- Mountain Heng (South) – the forehead
  南嶽衡山
- Mountain Song (Center) – the nose 中嶽嵩山
- Mountain Hua (West) – the right cheekbone
  西嶽華山
- Mountain Heng (North) – the chin and jaw
  北嶽恆山

The most important thing about the Five Mansions is that they're all balanced and proportionate. Combined with a balanced and even Cosmic Trinity, this already denotes the fortuitous potential for a happy and prosperous life.

The East and West Mountain should be high and even, the South Mountain should be broad, the North Mountain should be fleshy, and the Centre Mountain should be broad, upright, and strong.

Mountain Tai (East)

東嶽泰山

The Mountain Tai (East) refers to the area from the left cheekbone to the edge of the left ear. Both cheekbones govern a person's authority, power and overall fortune in life, particularly during middle age as was explained in the previous sections of this book. Specifically, the cheekbones govern the ages 46 and 47 for both men and women and are known as the 'Power Bones'.

Good or favourable cheekbones are those that are fleshy, and there should be no lines or scars cutting across them. Preferably, there should be no moles on the cheeks, either, or one directly on the cheekbones.

Good cheekbones accompanied by a well-developed nose indicates very good fortune, status and authority particularly around the ages 46 and 47. These fleshy cheekbones also denote a gentle, sentimental character who values friendship and community.

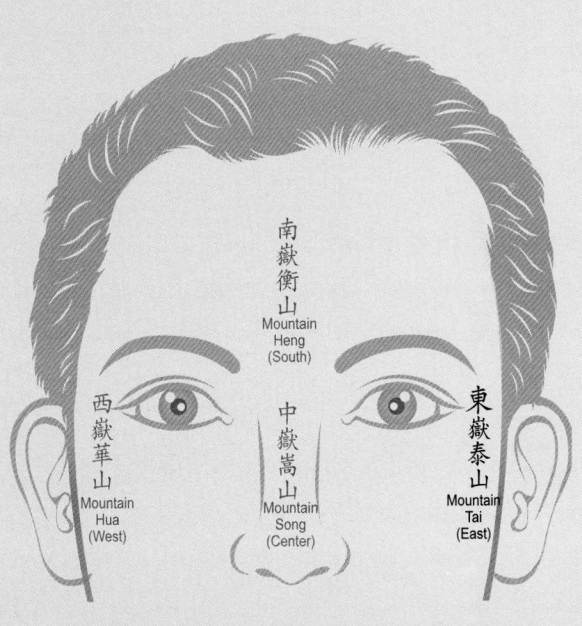

Mountain Heng (South) 南嶽衡山

The Mountain Heng (South) refers to the forehead. The forehead is one of the most important parts of the face because it contains five palaces: the Life, Career, Parents, Travelling, and Fortune and Virtue Palaces.

The forehead represents a person's professional outlook and career, as well as social status. A high, broad, and fleshy forehead is therefore desirable and ideal in terms of good prospects for career, intellect, talent, and capabilities, as well as for nobility.

Since it also denotes the formative or early experiences in one's life, it provides the clue for the foundational experiences of one's life which often gives a person a head start.

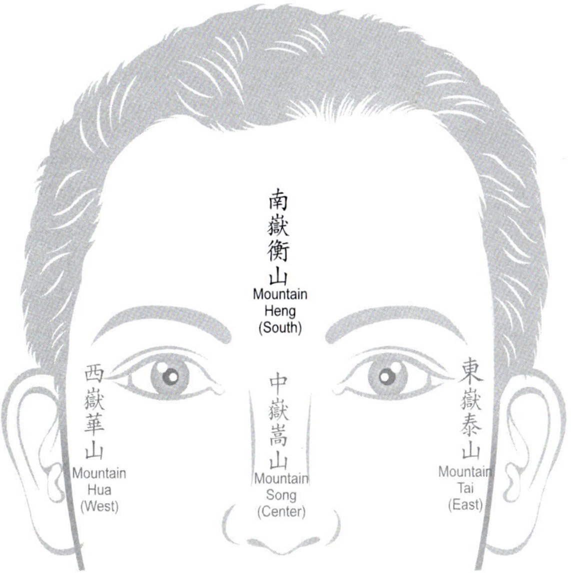

南嶽衡山
Mountain Heng (South)

西嶽華山
Mountain Hua (West)

中嶽嵩山
Mountain Song (Center)

東嶽泰山
Mountain Tai (East)

Mountain Song (Center)
中嶽嵩山

The Mountain Song (Center) refers to the nose. It is the central thing to consider when evaluating the Five Mountains, since the nose represents the Wealth Palace. To some extent, the Center Mountain also denotes a person's health and physical strength.

The nose tip, wings, and nostrils should be broad and fleshy, but the nostrils should not be so broad as to be up-turned, as this indicates a loss of wealth. The nose bridge should ideally be tall and straight, and the size of the nose should be good in relation to the rest of the face. A good nose denotes great abilities in amassing wealth.

A bony or crooked nose indicates a potentially defective character, while a too-thin nose or narrow nose, and pinched nostrils, indicate selfish personalities and the inability to earn or amass wealth. If the Center Mountain is not strong, it also denotes many failures in career.

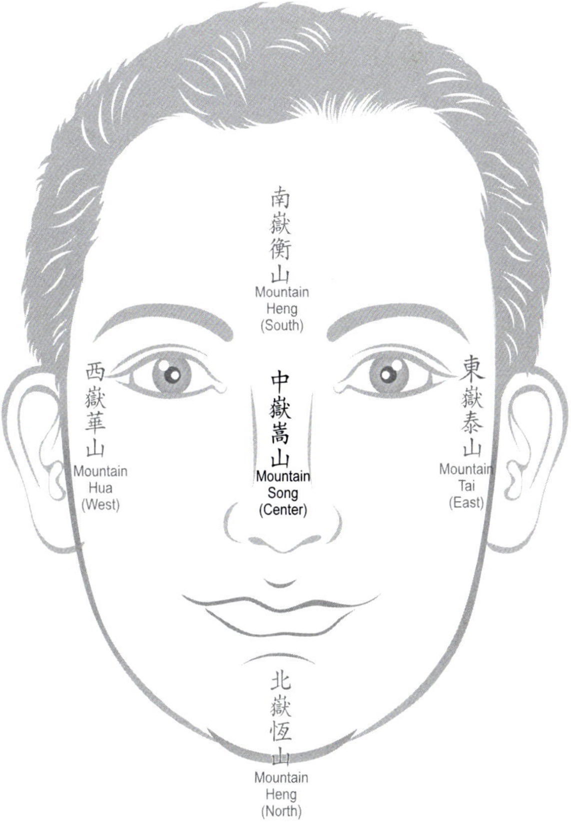

南嶽衡山
Mountain Heng (South)

西嶽華山
Mountain Hua (West)

中嶽嵩山
Mountain Song (Center)

東嶽泰山
Mountain Tai (East)

北嶽恆山
Mountain Heng (North)

宮位

Mountain Hua (West)
西嶽華山

The Mountain Hua (West) refers to the area from the right cheekbone to the edge of the right ear.

Good or strong cheekbones are necessary for status, power and authority. Fleshy cheeks denote good leadership. Bony cheekbones, on the other hand, belong to cold or ruthless individuals. These are people who will not stop at anything to get what they want.

Sagging cheekbones, or ones that droop, belong to uncharitable people and denote mean, somewhat cruel characters.

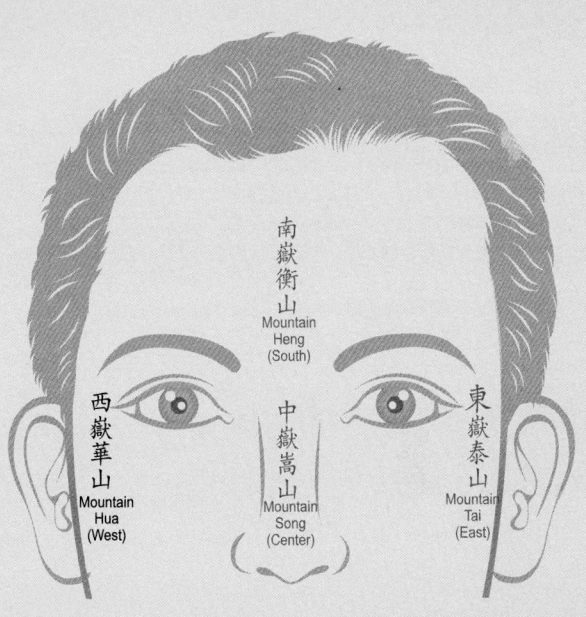

Mountain Heng (North) 北嶽恆山

The Mountain Heng (North) refers to the chin and jaw.

Being the lowest point of the face, this is also known as the Earth Corner. Ideally, it should be broad, fleshy, and gently rounded and protruding. This indicates that a person will enjoy great wealth, status, and respect in life and will never run out of love and support from family and friends in old age.

On a woman, in particular, a well-rounded Earth Corner indicates good home life and a caring nature. A square-shaped or sharp Earth Corner indicates a stubborn personality that may have to slog hard to make ends meet. The Mountain Heng and Earth Corner in particular should not be pointy or rough on the surface.

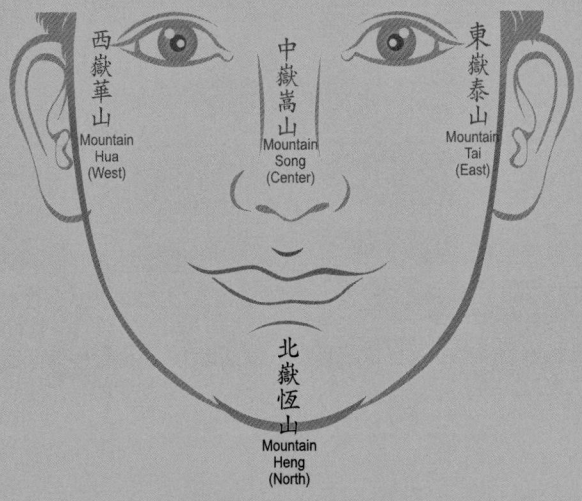

The Five Officers

The Five Officers 五官

The Five Officers is another key concept in Face Reading that serves as a crucial point of reference. The Five Officers can be summed up as:

- Eyes (the Vigilance Officer) 眼 – 監察官
- Ears (the Information Officer) 耳 – 採聽官
- Mouth (the Communications Officer) 口 – 出納官
- Nose (the Chief Justice Officer) 鼻 – 審辨官
- Eyebrows (the Insurance Officer) 眉 – 保壽官

The Eyes are known as the Vigilance Officer because the eyes reveals a person's perceptions of the world and the means by which people see and observe, while the ears are the Information Officer because it is tied to people's ability to listen and receive information.

The mouth is the Communications Officer because it is through the mouth that individuals communicate with each other, and as such it can reveal the quality of communication. The nose is the Chief Justice Officer because it governs and reveals a person's morals and sense of justice, as well as integrity. Finally, the eyebrows are known as the Insurance Officer because it reveals a person's quality of life in relation to character, longevity, and dignity.

Eyes – Vigilance Officer
眼 – 監察官

In Chinese metaphysics, the left eye represents the father, while the right eye represents the mother. The eyes represent a person's luck between the ages 35 to 40.

Eyes are also the Wealth Star. Good eyes are sharp, clear, and alert, with no discolouration. This indicates an intelligent person with good personal relationships. He or she has a positive mindset and is able to excel in his or her career.

The eyes can also reveal the essence of a person, and how one approaches life. Big eyes indicate emotional, sentimental people, while small eyes can denote a more austere, crafty personality.

Ears – Listening Officer
耳 – 採聽官

The definition of good ears includes well-defined ear ridges, thick, high-set, long, and broad, with a good color or tone definition. High-set ears with the tips of the ears (when seen from the front) that are higher than the eyebrows indicate intelligence.

The ears also denote a person's life luck from ages 1-14. The ears are also the Fortune Star, and if the ears are higher than the eyebrows as seen from the front, then one is likely to make one's fortune at a young age. However, if a person's ears are at the same level of the cheeks, then the wealth potential is likely to come during middle-age.

If the ear lobe is curved in towards the direction of the mouth, it indicates the likelihood that one is able to become very wealthy in old age. In terms of complexion color, if the ears are lighter-skinned than the rest of the face, it indicates possible fame. Reddish-toned ears denote wealth, as well.

Mouth – Information Officer 口 - 出納官

The mouth is also known as the Water Star. It indicates a person's luck between the ages of 51 and 63.

A good mouth can also denote how one is able to enjoy life – or the good life, such as it was. As such, a healthy reddish tint is something that is ideal in a good mouth. Both the upper and lower lips should be in proportion to each other. The lips should have clear definition and borders, and the corners should ideally point upwards even when a person is not smiling.

Good lips indicate good communication skills. It also represents good affinity with good food.

Thick lips tend to belong to those who are gentle and sentimental in nature, while thin lips reveals a person who is likely to be somewhat cold and calculating, with the ability to sweet-talk to get ahead.

宮位

Nose – Chief Justice Officer 鼻 – 審辨官

The Nose is also the Earth Star, and represents the Wealth Palace. It denotes a person's luck between the ages 41 and 50.

The nose is the root of wealth, and it is thus the key indicator of a person's ability to accumulate and amass wealth. A high, broad nose with a round tip and a stem that is broad and thick is a good nose. It should not be crooked or bony.

The nose tip is where one looks in order to gauge a wealth capacity (to keep money for the long-term), while the nose wings indicate the capacity to make money in the first place. Nostrils that are upturned are a bad sign, as it denotes loss of wealth.

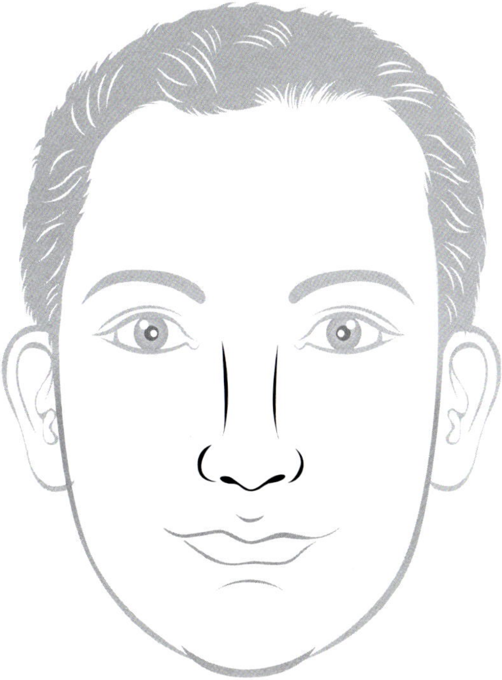

Eyebrows – Insurance Officer 眉 – 保壽官

The eyebrows indicate a person's luck between the ages 31 and 34, and it is also the Siblings Palace.

Eyebrows should be noted for its length, direction of hair growth, and thickness or density of the eyebrows. Eyebrows that are longer than the eyes indicate that the person may have more than four siblings.

Moderate, uniform and neat growth of hair indicates a person who enjoys good ties with his or her siblings, and who has a general organised and disciplined way in life. Chips or breaks in the eyebrows indicate that the person's siblings may have significant. health problems.

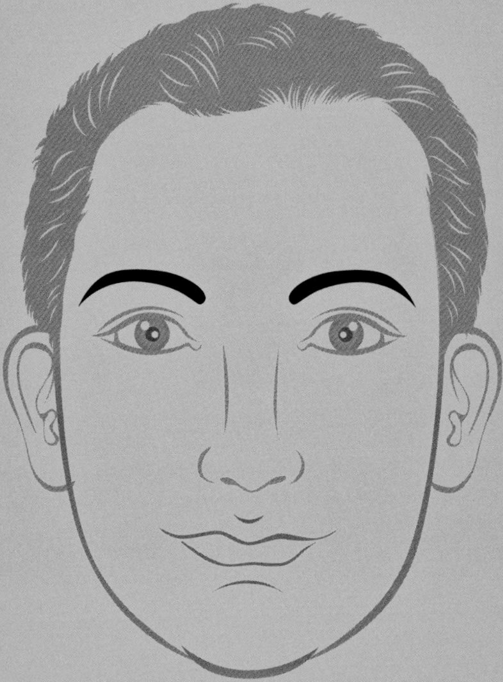

宮位

The FOUR RIVERS

The Four Rivers 四瀆

As Face Reading is an aspect of Physiognomy in Chinese metaphysics, the metaphors of mountains and rivers are also used to explain the landscape of the face. As such, The Four Rivers refer to the face's Five Officers – namely, the ears, eyes, mouth, and nose. The ears are known as Rivers and the eyes as Streams, while the mouth is known as the Creek and the nose as Canal.

The Four Rivers, as you may have deduced from the name, all pertain to bodies of water. In metaphysics and in physiognomy, the Mountains represent Yin while Water represents Yang. As such, when evaluating the Four Rivers we look for what makes for good or favourable aspects of the Water element. Water should be clear and running smoothly, without impediment, as opposed to being murky, clogged, or stagnant.

As such, the flow of the Rivers is essential. If, in evaluating the Four Rivers, it appears to be healthy, clear, and smooth-flowing, this denotes health, positivity, prosperity, and longevity.

Ears – Rivers 耳爲江瀆

The ears represent a person's immune system and physical health and ability; intelligence and IQ; luck in senior age; and lives from the ages 1 to 14.

Good ears are well-developed and well-defined, with clear ridges. This means that this is a person who is blessed with a good start in life between the ages of 1 to 14 that can bring about future success.

It will also be good for the ear passage to be wide and deep, and the ear itself to feel strong to the touch yet firm. This indicates good fortune. The ears also define a person's mental and emotional state.

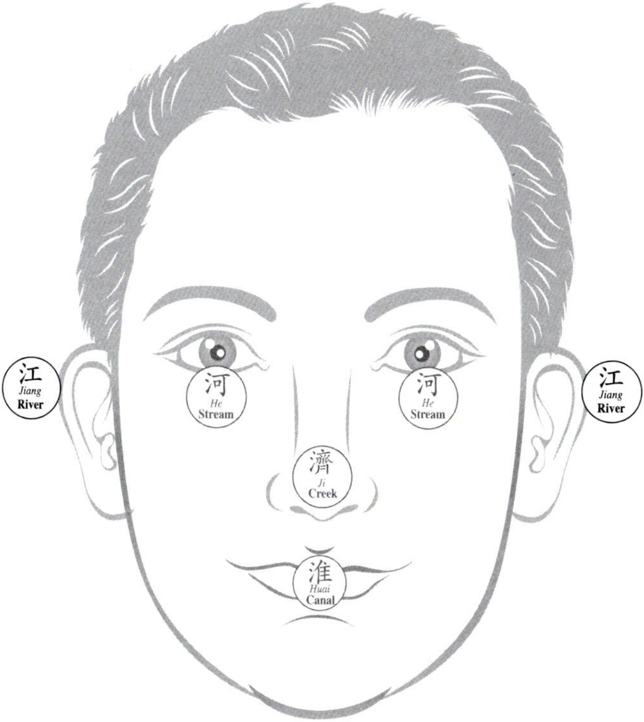

Eyes – Streams 目爲河瀆

The eyes represent a person's intentions and true characters, which is why people tend to associate the essence of a 'soul' as seen through the eyes.

Ideal eyes should be long, almost almond-shaped, with a slight tilt upwards towards the end. The whites should be clear, and the clarity and tone should be bright. This represents nobility, and it also indicates good health.

Furthermore, the eye 'spirit' as it's referred to in Face Reading should be sharp, alert, and quick – indicating a brilliant mind and those who are able to act fast. Gloomy or watery eyes indicate slow movers, while dull or tired-looking eyes indicate problems and bad fortune.

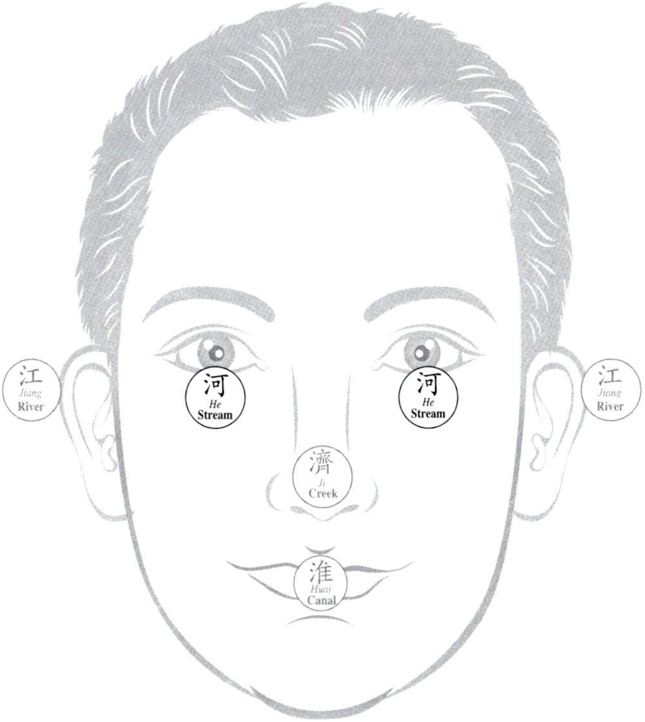

江 Jiang River　河 He Stream　河 He Stream　江 Jiang River

濟 Ji Creek

淮 Huai Canal

宮位

Mouth – the Canal
口爲淮瀆

The mouth is the most prominent of the Five Officers and indicates a person's ability to communicate, and the quality and shape of the mouth denotes one's quality of communication.

The ideal mouth should be generous or fairly large, and almost square-shaped with well-defined borders and curves. The lips should preferably have a healthy rosy sheen and the corners of the mouth should tilt up even when the mouth is closed and unsmiling.

Lips should be symmetrical, and not off-balance or crooked, as this indicates a person who uses words for improper ends or with double meaning.

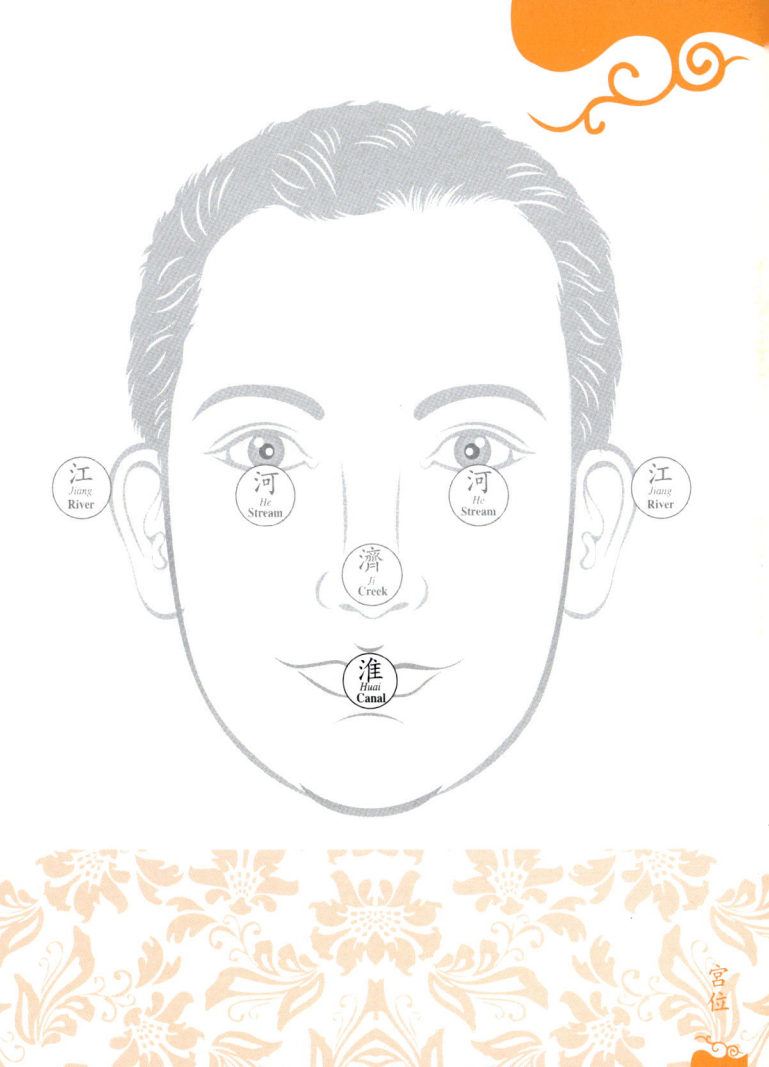

Nose – the Creek
鼻爲濟瀆

The nose is a good indicator of a person's sense of self and confidence, as well as his or her sense of integrity.

A nose should ideally be straight and charismatic, the latter meaning that is prominent (approximately 1/3 of the face), fleshy, and firm. A too-small nose indicates someone who might be prone to being subservient to others and playing second-fiddle.

A sharp, pointy, or hooked nose denotes a similarly sharp character with possible ill-intentions, while a crooked or bent nose denotes a crooked personality.

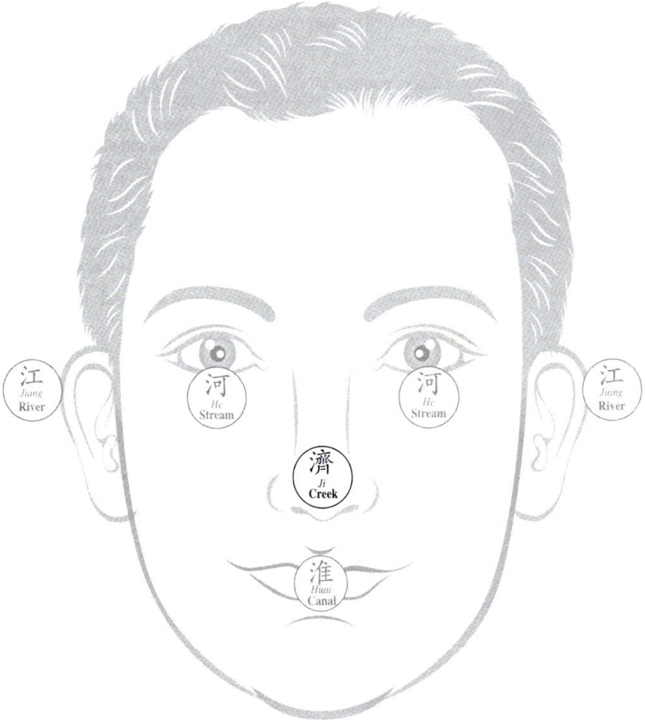
江
Jiang
River
河
He
Stream
河
He
Stream
江
Jiang
River
濟
Ji
Creek
淮
Huai
Canal

The FIVE STARS

Metal Star – Right Ear
金星 – 右耳

The Metal Star is identified by the right ear. What makes a good Metal Star is the same factors that makes Metal good – density, thickness, and a pure unalloyed color or tone of the flesh.

The Metal Star will be even more auspicious if the Pearl in the Ear is present. The Pearl in the Ear formation, indicates optimism and a happy-go-lucky personality.

This indicates a person who usually approaches the world as half-full instead of half-empty, and denotes a person who strives to fulfill obligations instead of passively waiting for opportunities. As such, an ideal Metal Ear formation can denote good fortune, prosperity, and longevity.

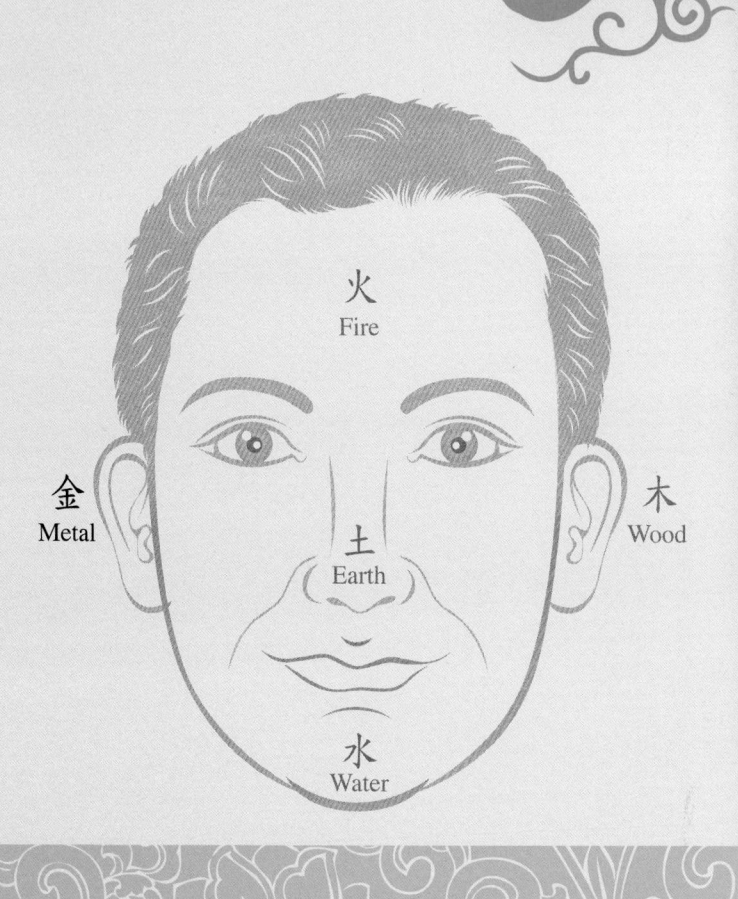

Wood Star – Left Ear
木星 – 左耳

The Wood Star is identified by the left ear. Like the Metal Star, a Wood star should be firm but yielding to the touch, and preferably thick and broad instead of crinkly or limp.

The Wood Star will similarly be more auspicious if the Pearl in the Ear formation is present.

The positive traits of the Wood Star are similar to the Metal Star.

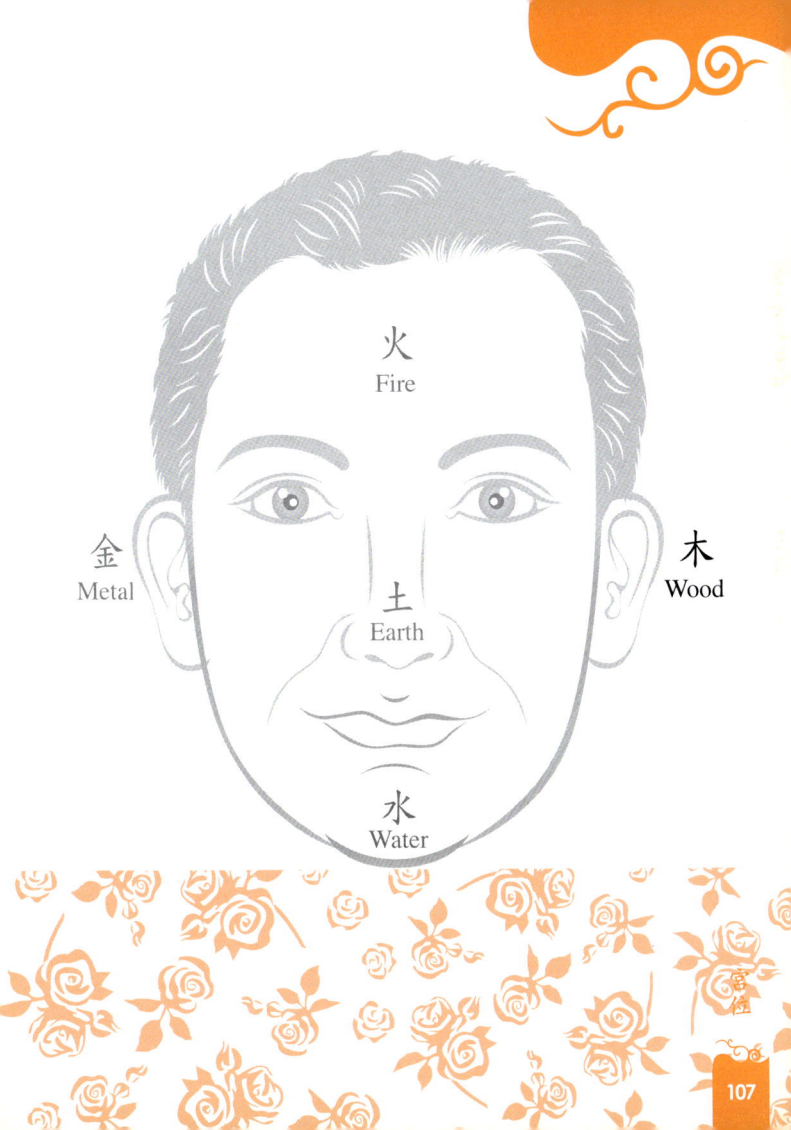

Water Star – Mouth
水星 – 口啊

The Water Star is identified by the mouth, which is also one of the Five Officers of the face.

A good mouth is one that is defined by red, symmetrical, and well-shaped lips as well as white, healthy straight teeth.

A well-balanced, symmetrical mouth is one where both upper and lower lips are of equal size denote a trustworthy, reliable person whose speech is elegant and precise. Because he or she is able to communicate well with people of all levels, this person is also likely to possess authority and integrity.

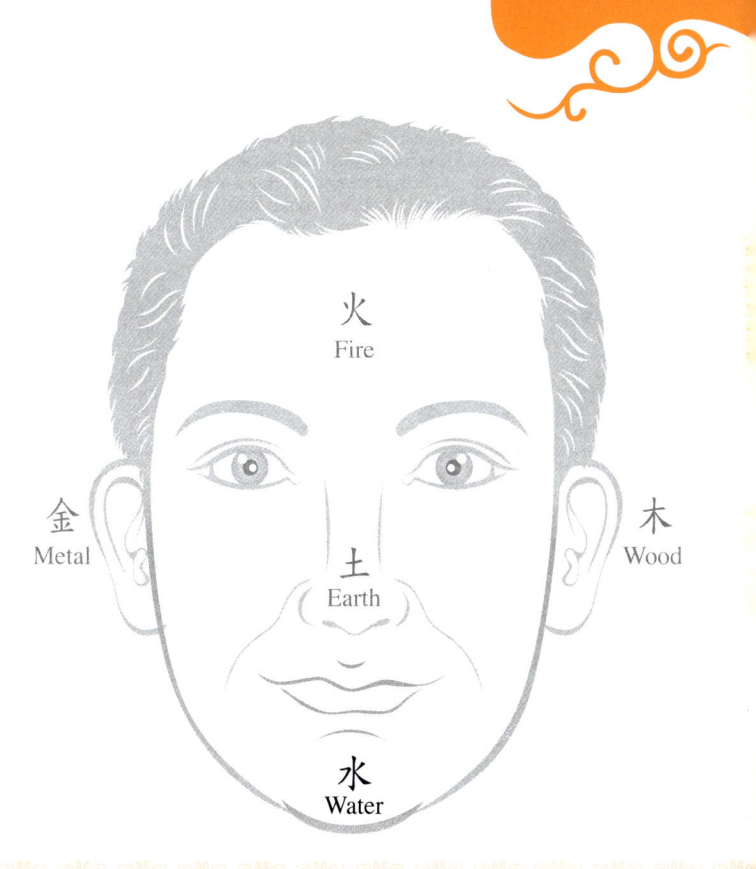

Fire Star – Forehead
火星 － 額

The Fire Star denotes the forehead. An ideal forehead is broad, wide, and spacious, and fleshy with a full appearance instead of sunken or concave.

Since the forehead denotes wisdom as well, a good forehead can indicate excellent career and wealth luck because one is able to harness talents and intelligence for success.

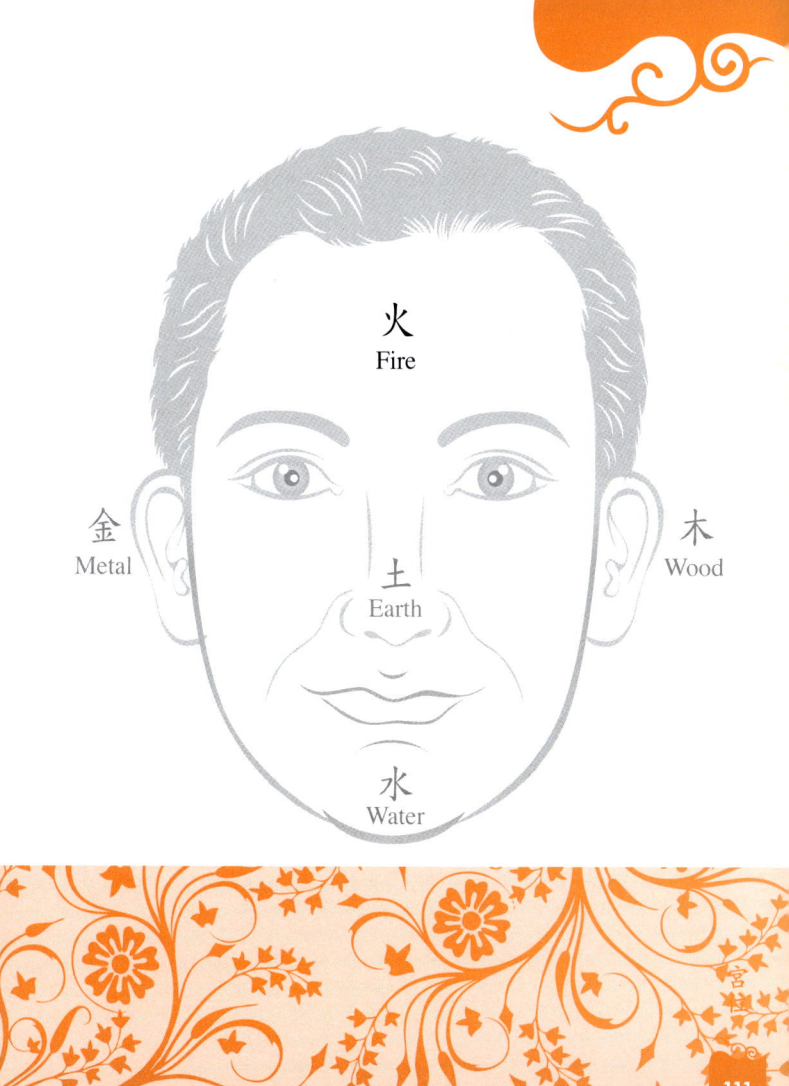

Earth Star – Nose
土星 － 鼻

The Earth Star denotes the nose, which is also one of the crucial Five Officers of the face.

A good nose is one that is fleshy, high-set, and relatively broad in comparison to the rest o the face. It is also necessary that the nose is straight. The nose wings should be full, as well, but the nostrils should not be exposed.

In this case, a good nose or Earth Star can denote prosperity, and if the nose also indicates an ability to retain wealth, then it can also mean good health. A good Earth Star denotes a stable character.

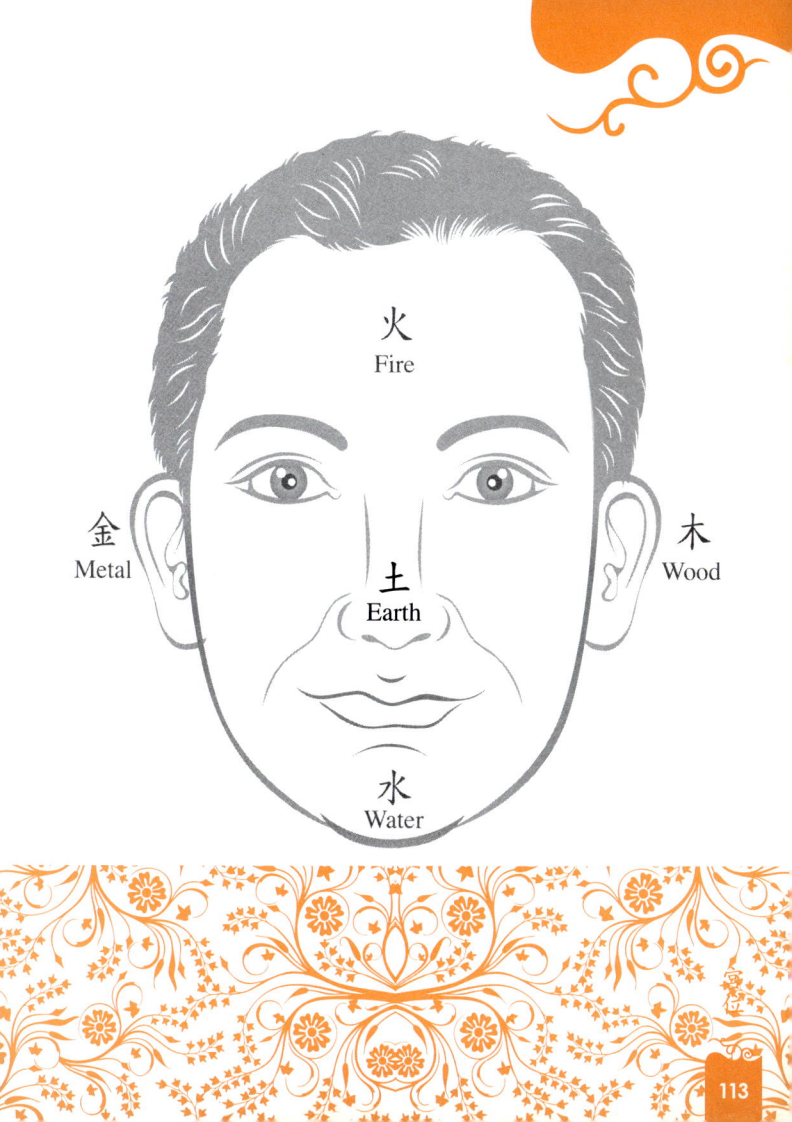

SIX BRIGHTNESS
六曜

The Six Brightness refers to two out of the Five Officers of the face, specifically the eyes and the eyebrows, and the also the forehead region. The latter essentially consists of the Life Palace and the Mountain Root.

The Six Brightness comprise Zi Qi (Purple Qi), Yue Bei (Moon Polo), Luo Hou (Rahu), Ji Duo (Ketu), and Great Yang and Great Yin.

Zi Qi (Purple Qi) 紫氣

This denotes the Resource Hall, which also known as the Life Palace. This is located right between the eyebrows.

The Resource Hall is a significant reference point for Face Reading for both men and women. This is because it provides a reading for one's life in general, in terms of good and bad. A good Resource Hall denotes if one's life can be fairly smooth-sailing with minimal difficulties, and can reveal if a person is sincere, generous, and open-minded, or the reverse.

As such, a Resource Hall should be fleshy, flat, and broad.

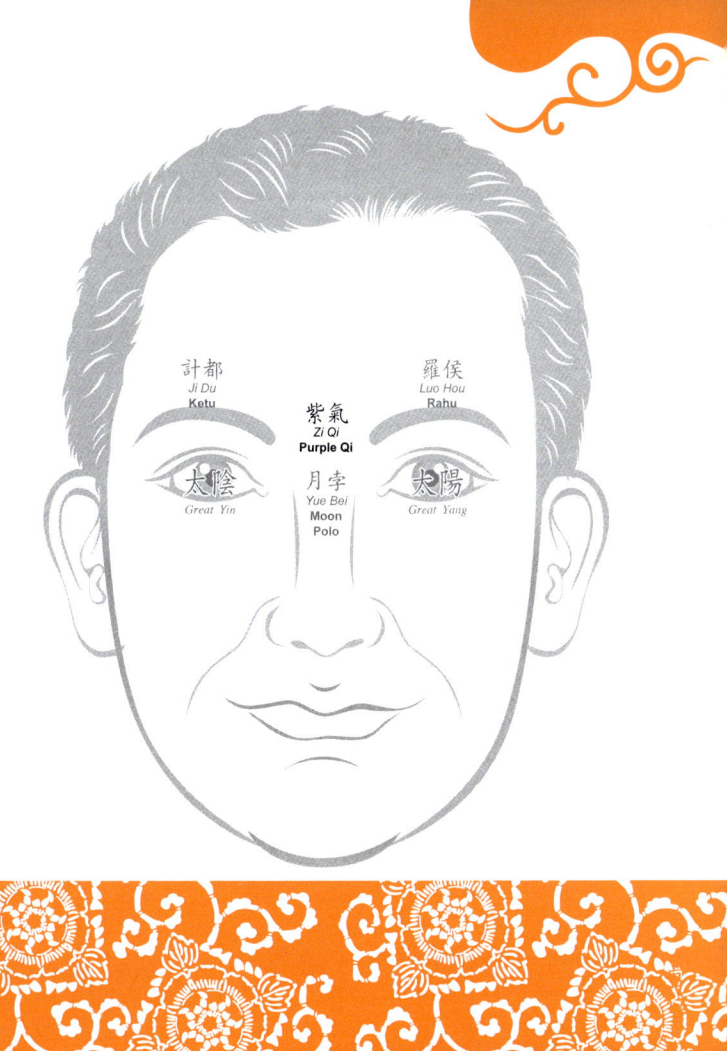

Yue Bei (Moon Polo)
月孛

This represents the Mountain Root, which is also the Health Palace.

The Mountain Root, which is located between the eyes, all the way down until the central axis of the face to the tip of the nose, governs the ages between 41 and 50. A favourable Mountain Root is one that is fleshy, broad, and high, as opposed to low or sunken.

There should not be lines, scars, or blemishes on the Mountain Root. This denotes poor health and/or the presence of significant illness. A good Mountain Root also denotes the help of Noble People.

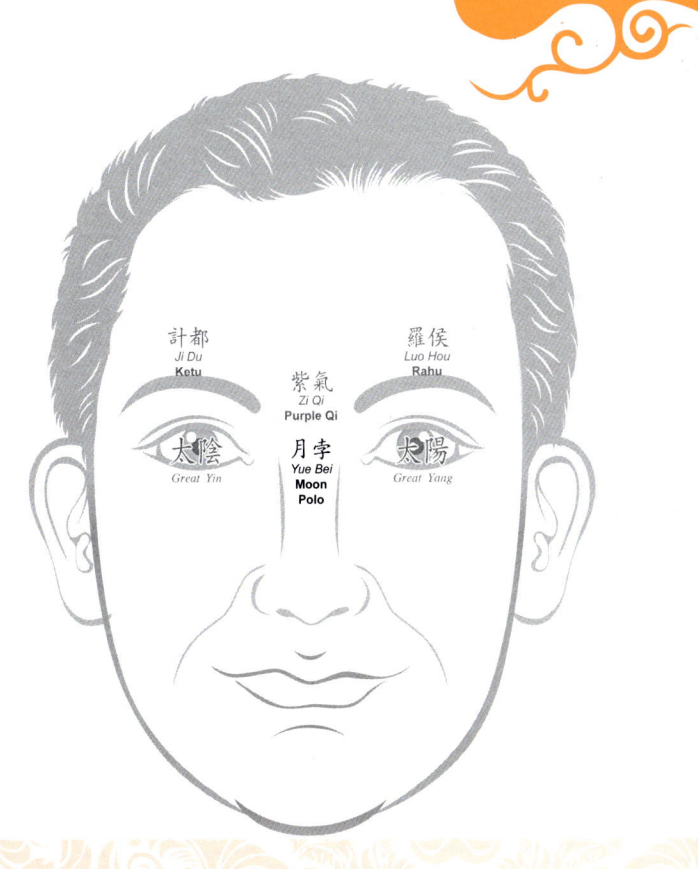

Luo Hou (Rahu) 羅喉

This represents the left eyebrow. Brow Luck refers to a person's luck and life and represents the ages between 31 and 34.

Ideal eyebrows should thus be neat and with moderate density and thickness, with eyebrow hair that grows in a steady, uniform direction.

Where this is found, the person will always receive help and support from siblings or partners.

The eyebrows can also represent one's career during those ages and thus denotes a person's capacity for success.

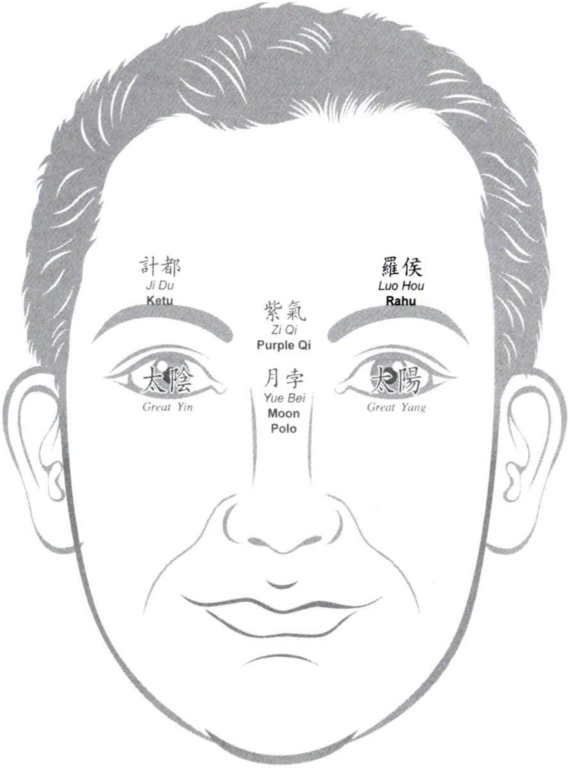

計都
Ji Du
Ketu

羅侯
Luo Hou
Rahu

紫氣
Zi Qi
Purple Qi

太陰
Great Yin

月孛
Yue Bei
Moon
Polo

太陽
Great Yang

宮位

Ji Duo (Ketu) 計都

This represents the right eyebrow.

The criteria for assessing the Ji Duo are similar to the criteria for Luo Hou. Where eyebrows are concerned, as well, it should be necessary that there is at least a finger's width of space separating the eye from the brow.

This is because low-set eyebrows set close to the eyes tend to suppress the Property Palace (which is the space between the eye and eyebrow), and thus renders the Property Palace unfavourable for the person. For men, a suppressed Property Palace can also mean one who is overly subservient to a domineering wife.

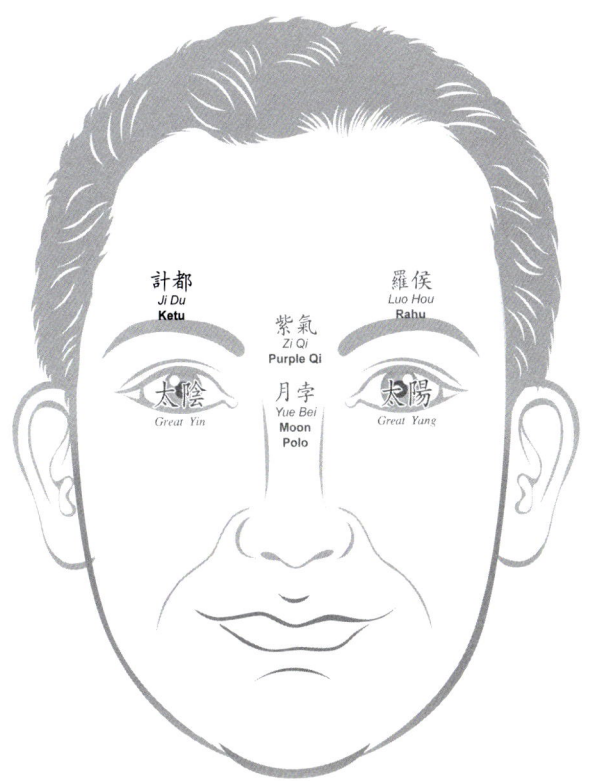

123

Great Yang and Great Yin

太陽太陰

Great Yang represents the left eye, while Great Yin represents the right eye.

Both Great Yang and Great Yin denote the pupils of the eyes, and eyes, if you remember, constitute one of the Five Officers of the face.

The pupils and the whites of the eyes should be clearly defined, and clear, with a good eye-spirit that indicates brightness and alertness. This denotes someone who is experiencing good fortune and smooth-sailing. If the pupils and the whites of the eyes are not clearly defined or appear blurry/vague, then the person is likely to face quite a lot of obstacles and may have burdens wearing him or her down.

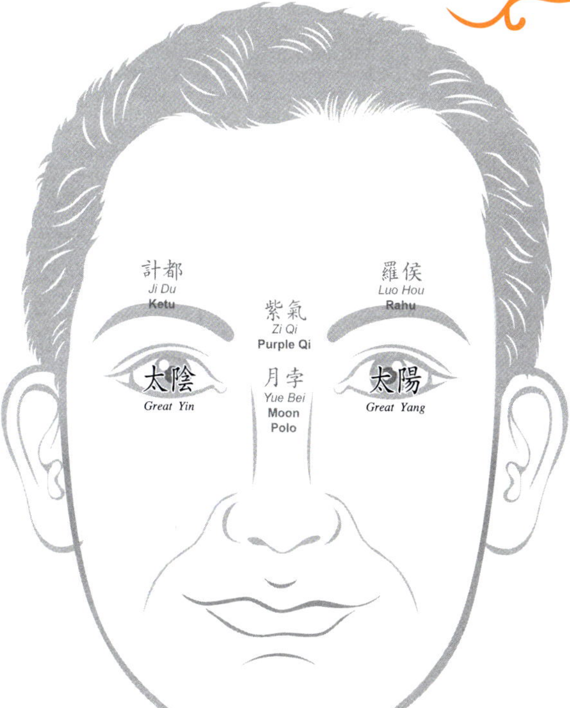

計都
Ji Du
Ketu

羅侯
Luo Hou
Rahu

紫氣
Zi Qi
Purple Qi

太陰
Great Yin

月孛
Yue Bei
Moon Polo

太陽
Great Yang

The Four Academic Halls
四學堂

The Four Academic Halls comprise:

- Officer Academic Hall, as represented by the eyes
- Prosperous Academic Hall, as represented by the forehead
- Internal Academic Hall, as represented by the teeth
- External Academic Hall, as represented by the ears

The Officer Academic Hall – Eyes 官學堂

To assess how the eyes relate to the Officer Academic Hall, pay attention to the movement of the eyes. Honest people will tend to look at others straight in the eye, and their gaze will appear clear and sharp. This is also the hallmark of good communication.

On the other hand, a person who can't look someone in the eye is probably hiding something, or may be suffering from lack of confidence. Shifty eyes or people who blink a lot may also denote the same things, as do wandering or roving eyes and eyes that furtively dart about.

Eyes should preferably long in width, reasonably wide, and clear. As such, since the eyes are also known as the Officer Stars, this denotes authority and status.

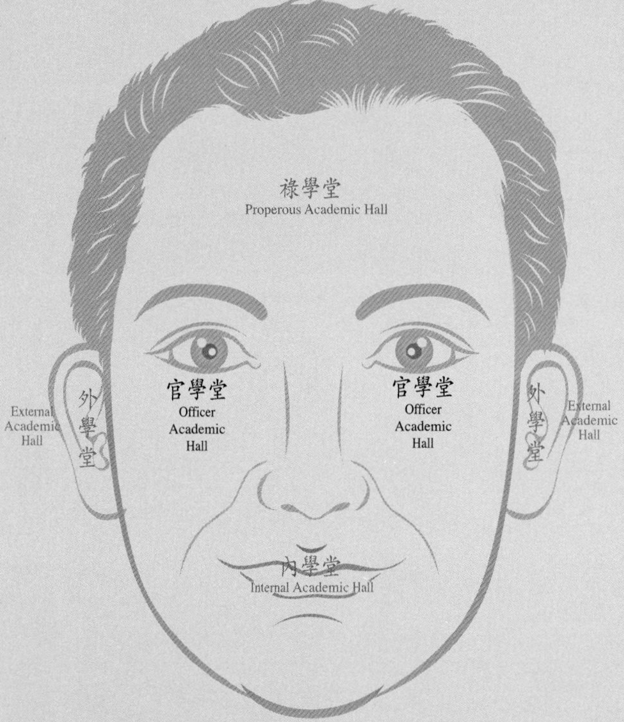

祿學堂
Properous Academic Hall

官學堂
Officer Academic Hall

官學堂
Officer Academic Hall

外學堂
External Academic Hall

外學堂
External Academic Hall

內學堂
Internal Academic Hall

官位

The Prosperous Academic Hall – Forehead 祿學堂

The forehead that is broad, full and high with a clear complexion tend to be the best in terms of assessing it in relation to the Prosperous Academic Hall.

A person's forehead should preferably not have any scars or dents across it, and it should not be uneven with bumps. A broad, high, and smooth forehead augurs well for intelligence and capability, and hence it is good for activities related to money-making, i.e. prosperity.

Entrepreneurs and business people with a good forehead will have better career and wealth luck, and they are likely to last longer in their industry because a good Prosperous Academic Hall also denotes lasting success and longevity.

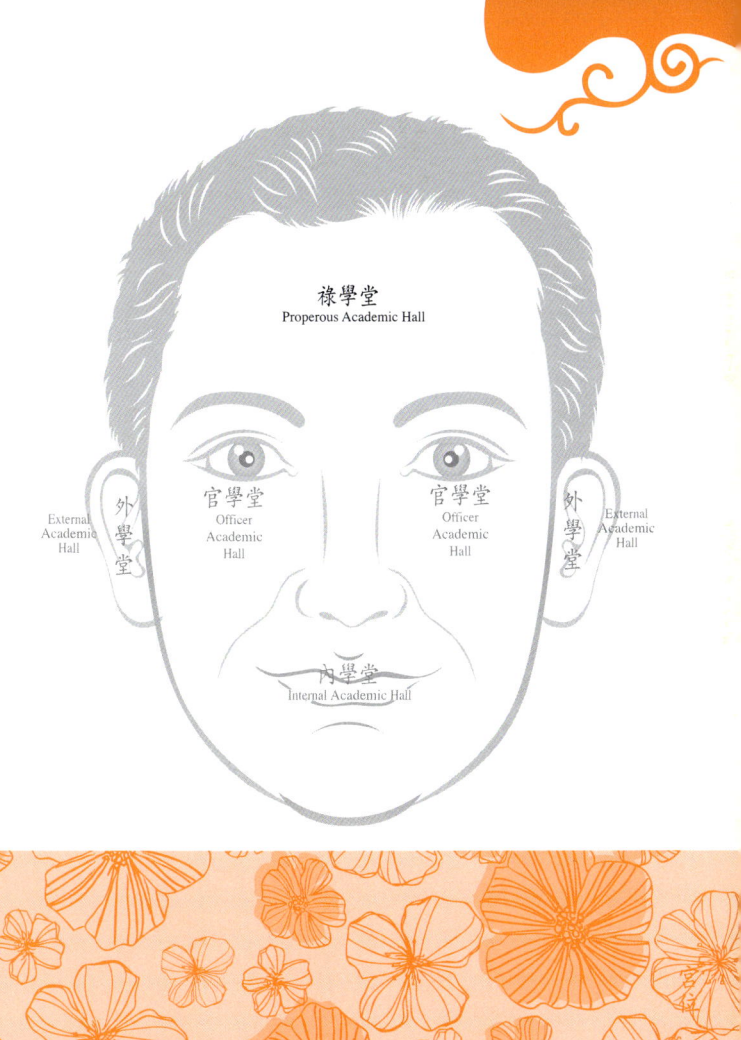

The Internal Academic Hall – Teeth 內學堂

The teeth is considered the Internal Academic Hall because it is usually concealed by the lips, and thus not immediately revealed (most times) at first glance.

The front teeth should be straight and white as well as neatly arranged without gaps – this indicates that a person is capable of being loyal and respectful to others. Sharp, pointy teeth denote a person who is overly assertive to the point of rudeness. Protruding teeth denotes a person who may rub others the wrong way by constantly saying the wrong thing at the wrong time.

To augur well as the Internal Academic Hall, teeth should be straight, well-balanced, and even, while appearing tidy and close-set without gaps or dents. This indicates a sincere character whose words mean well and reflect a good heart.

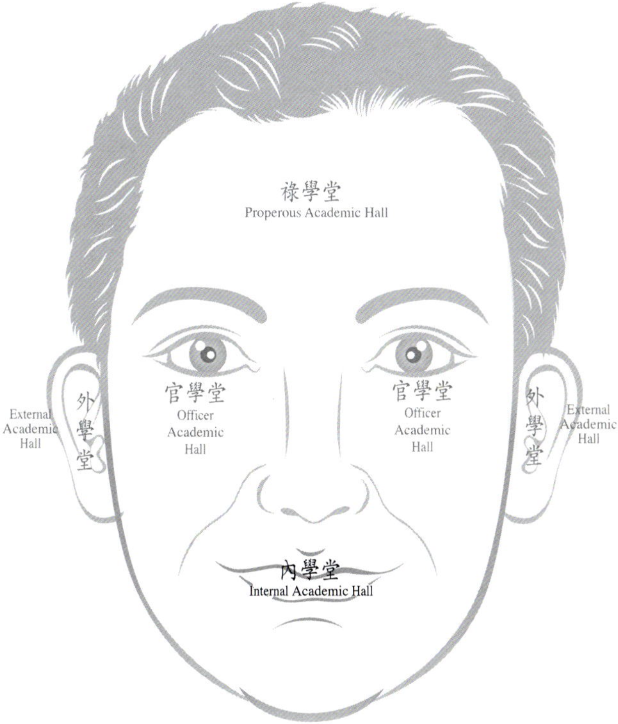

祿學堂
Properous Academic Hall

官學堂
Officer Academic Hall

官學堂
Officer Academic Hall

外學堂
External Academic Hall

外學堂
External Academic Hall

內學堂
Internal Academic Hall

The External Academic Hall – Ears
外學堂

The ears are the External Academic Hall because it situated on the 'outside' and takes in information.

When evaluating the ears, it's important to take note of the setting of the ears (high), the symmetry of the ears (when seen from the front), the flexibility of the ears (not too hard, not too soft and limp), the rims or borders of the ears (well-defined, preferably broad), the shells of the ears (clearly-defined), and the wind-gaps of the ears (also broad).

Ears are best when fleshy and full, as well as high-set, because it denotes full intelligence and good luck in life. The colour or flesh-tone of the ears should also be bright and preferably lighter than the tone of the face, instead of darker.

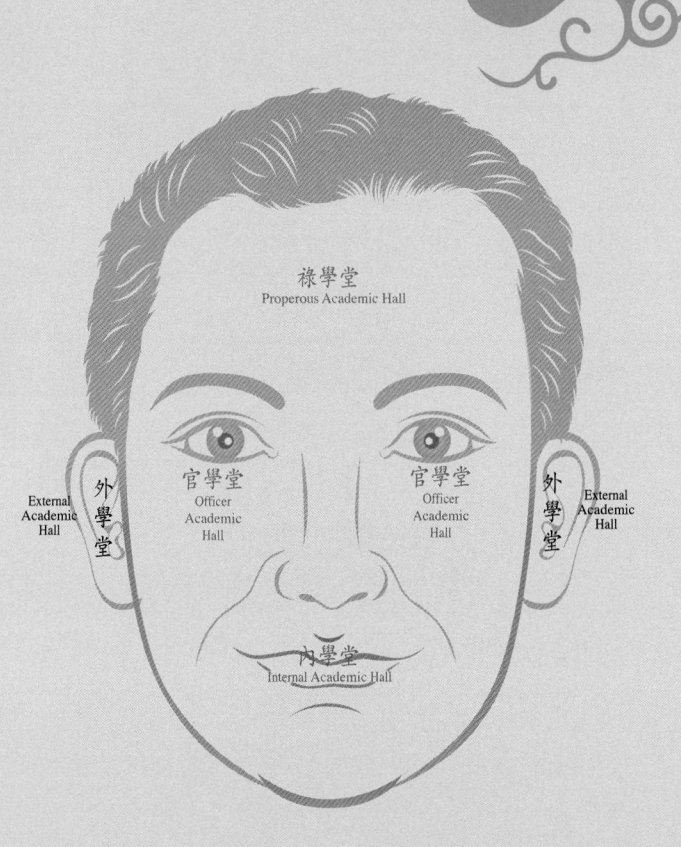

The Eight Academic Halls
八學堂

The Eight Academic Halls of the face comprise:

- High Bright Academic Hall 高明學堂
- High Broad Academic Hall 高廣學堂
- Bamboo-Shoot Level Academic Hall 班筍學堂
- Big Bright Academy Hall 光大學堂
- Elegant Academic Hall 明秀學堂
- Loyal Academic Hall 忠信學堂
- High Broad Academic Hall 高廣學堂
- Intelligent Academic Hall 聰明學堂

An important point for ascertaining each Hall is to note its qualities: it must be fleshy, plump and clear in complexion and possess clarity. This will indicate great intelligence and wisdom.

On the other hand, sunken, gloomy and or untidy Halls hint at a lack of knowledge or wisdom as well as denoting a poor character.

The High Bright Academic Hall
高明學堂

The High Bright Academic Hall denotes the top of the forehead.

Ideally, the High Bright Academic Hall should be round-shaped, full, and without bone protrusion. This indicates good memory and analytical prowess.

A rounded head that is coupled with a high forehead also augurs well for intelligence and wealth management capabilities.

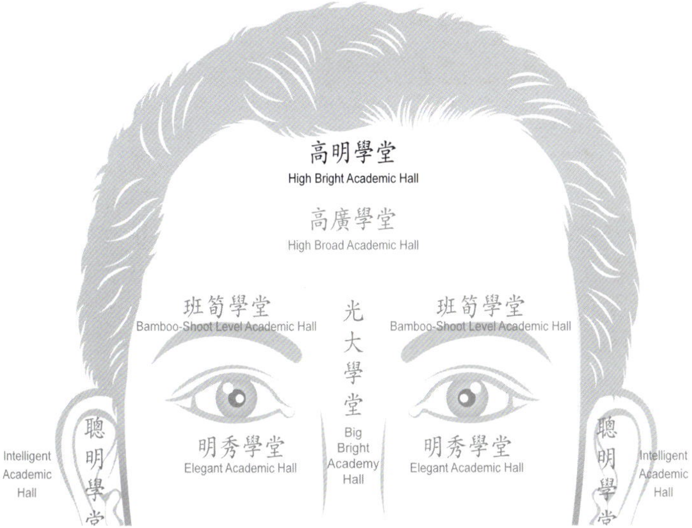

高明學堂
High Bright Academic Hall

高廣學堂
High Broad Academic Hall

班筍學堂
Bamboo-Shoot Level Academic Hall

光大學堂
Big Bright Academy Hall

班筍學堂
Bamboo-Shoot Level Academic Hall

聰明學堂
Intelligent Academic Hall

明秀學堂
Elegant Academic Hall

明秀學堂
Elegant Academic Hall

聰明學堂
Intelligent Academic Hall

宮位

The High Broad Academic Hall
高廣學堂

The High Broad Academic Hall denotes the corners or fringes of the forehead, bordering the hairline.

A person's overall luck and fortune in life can be ascertained from looking at the High Broad Academic Hall. The edges of the forehead should preferably be full and flat in appearance, as opposed to bony or pointy or sunken.

It should also be clear and flawless, and with a square-like shape that indicates evenness. This denotes well for a person's affinity with elders and mentors. A good High Broad Academic Hall belongs to a person who has strong, powerful connections.

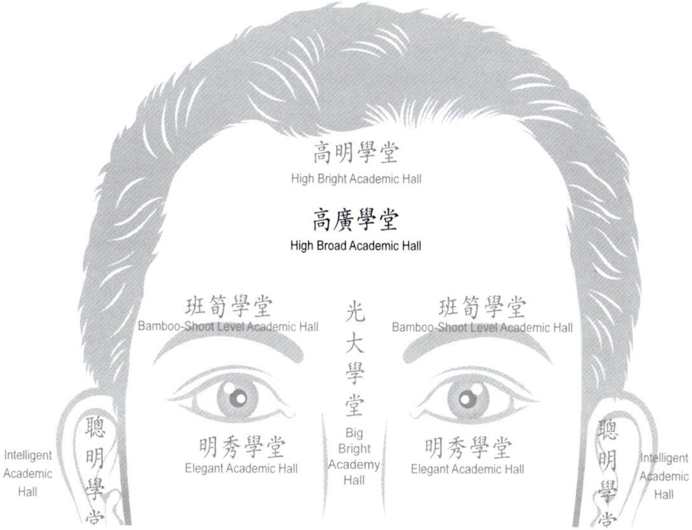

高明學堂
High Bright Academic Hall

高廣學堂
High Broad Academic Hall

班筍學堂
Bamboo-Shoot Level Academic Hall

光大學堂
Big Bright Academy Hall

班筍學堂
Bamboo-Shoot Level Academic Hall

聰明學堂
Intelligent Academic Hall

明秀學堂
Elegant Academic Hall

明秀學堂
Elegant Academic Hall

聰明學堂
Intelligent Academic Hall

官位

The Big Bright Academic Hall
光大學堂

The Big Bright Academic Hall is also the Resource Hall.

The Big Bright Academic Hall also governs the quality of one's career prospects and wealth luck. Therefore, it should be firm and full, with clear skin tone and no blemishes or scars. Ideally, it should also appear flat and without bumps.

This position also shows one's ability to learn a new skill quickly.

When it has these positive traits, then the Big Bright Academic Hall also denotes strong career luck.

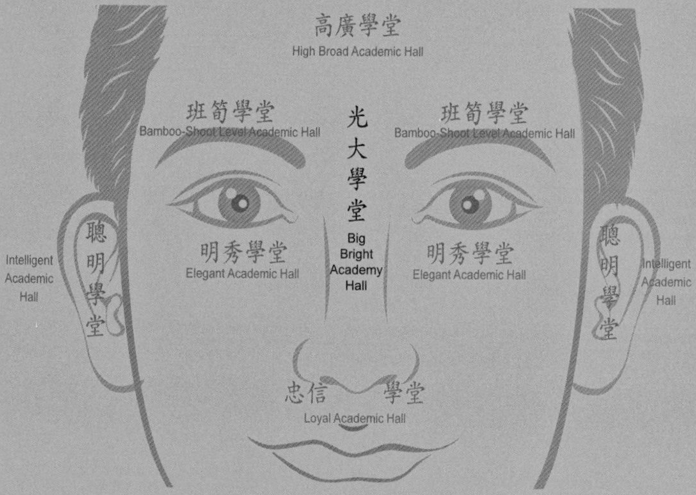

高廣學堂
High Broad Academic Hall

班筍學堂
Bamboo-Shoot Level Academic Hall

光大學堂
Big Bright Academy Hall

班筍學堂
Bamboo-Shoot Level Academic Hall

聰明學堂
Intelligent Academic Hall

明秀學堂
Elegant Academic Hall

明秀學堂
Elegant Academic Hall

聰明學堂
Intelligent Academic Hall

忠信　學堂
Loyal Academic Hall

宮位

The Elegant Academic Hall 明秀學堂

The Elegant Academic Hall is represented by the eyes.

As such, the eyes should ideally be long and elegant-looking, with a fine and gentle curve or uplift towards the end.

A person's sense of nobility and character, as well as intelligence, can be gauged from the eyes. As such, it is ideal if the eyes are clear, balanced, and if a person has a frank and direct gaze.

Where this is found, the person has exceptional ability to communicate with the opposite sex. He or she will enjoy good relationships and love luck.

Murky or muddy-looking eyes, or even discoloured eyes, and eyes that shift about too much or stare vaguely into space tend to hint at characters that are hiding something or lacking alertness and intelligence.

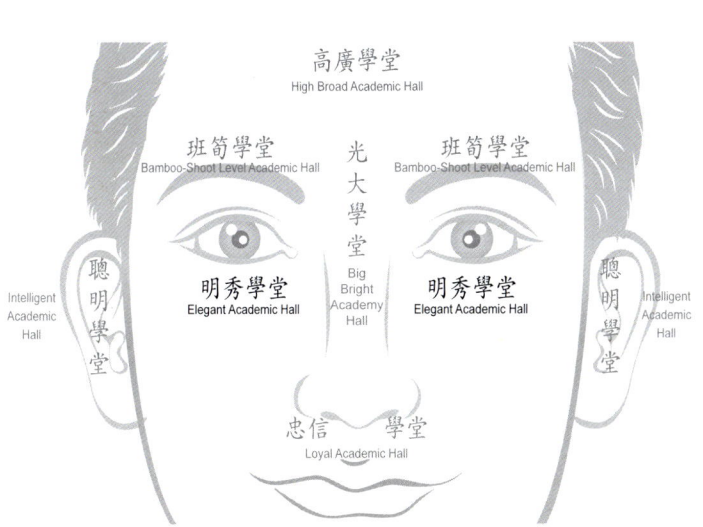

The Intelligent Academic Hall
聰明學堂

The Intelligent Academic Hall is represented by the ears.

The ears are best when it is thick, long, even-coloured and bright in skin tone and clarity, and with clear, well-shaped and well-defined ridges and shells.

Besides revealing intelligence, the ears can also reveal a person's social standing or status. In this sense, ears can denote a person's capacity for fame or reputation, and ears that possess the good features mentioned above represent people who are likely to enjoy some measure of fame.

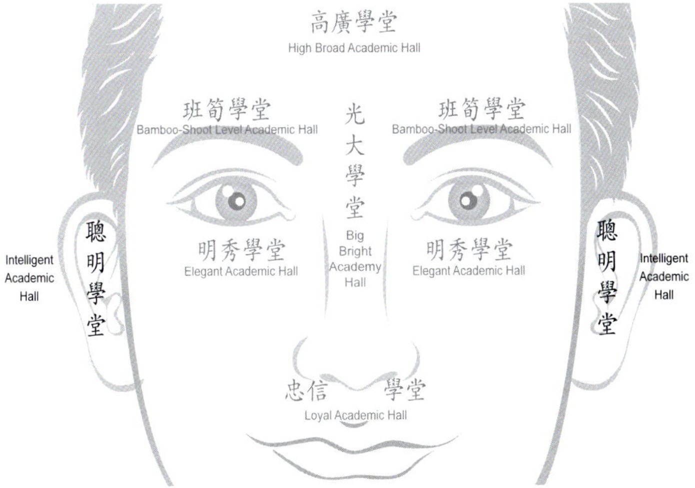

學堂

- 高廣學堂 High Broad Academic Hall
- 班筍學堂 Bamboo-Shoot Level Academic Hall
- 光大學堂 Big Bright Academy Hall
- 明秀學堂 Elegant Academic Hall
- 聰明學堂 Intelligent Academic Hall
- 忠信學堂 Loyal Academic Hall

宮位

The Loyal Academic Hall 忠信學堂

The Loyal Academic Hall is represented by the mouth.

This Hall indicates the level of prosperity one is able to enjoy in life. The mouth should thus be ideally well-balanced and bordered by healthy-looking, even-sized lips.

This position also reveals whether this person has many or any loyal subjects or friends.

Furthermore, the mouth should open to reveal tidy, even teeth that is not too large or small. This denotes good prosperity and fortune.

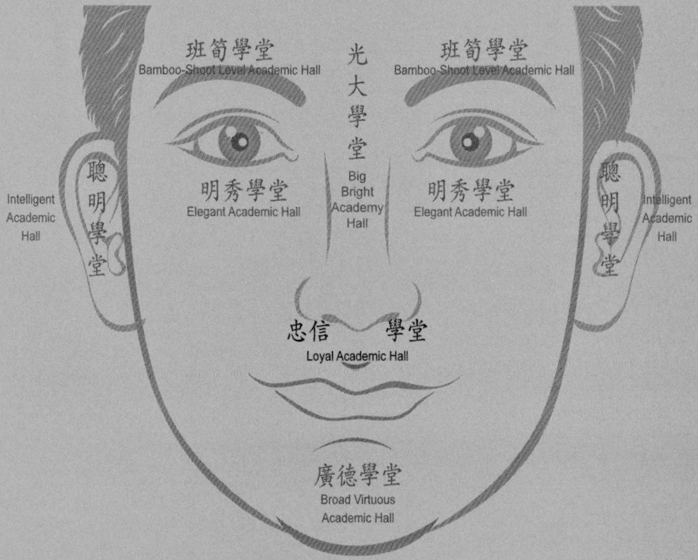

班筍學堂
Bamboo-Shoot Level Academic Hall

光大學堂
Big Bright Academy Hall

班筍學堂
Bamboo-Shoot Level Academic Hall

聰明學堂
Intelligent Academic Hall

明秀學堂
Elegant Academic Hall

明秀學堂
Elegant Academic Hall

聰明學堂
Intelligent Academic Hall

忠信　學堂
Loyal Academic Hall

廣德學堂
Broad Virtuous Academic Hall

宮位

149

The Broad Virtuous Academic Hall
廣德學堂

The Broad Virtuous Academic Hall is represented by the tongue.

Admittedly, studying the tongue is not easy since it is rarely revealed long enough to be subject to scrutiny! However, the tongue is a good indicator of a person's sense of integrity.

The ideal tongue should be long, not short and stubby, and should be a healthy reddish-pink in color throughout. A healthy tongue denotes honest, trustworthy individuals, who speaks well of others.

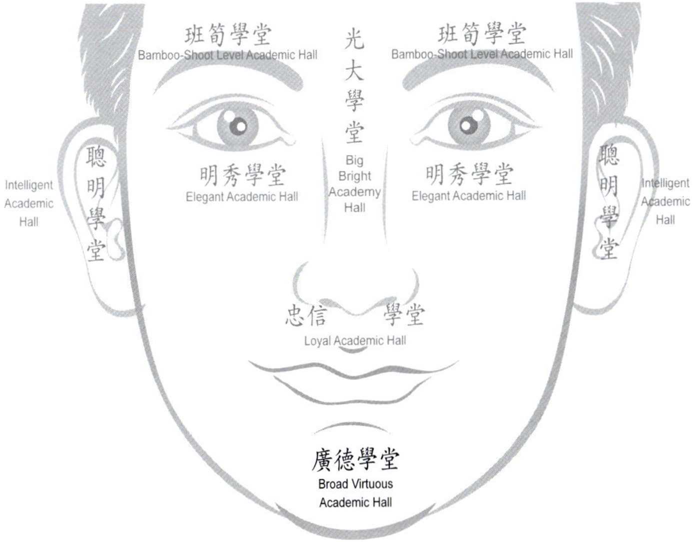

班筍學堂 Bamboo-Shoot Level Academic Hall
班筍學堂 Bamboo-Shoot Level Academic Hall
光大學堂 Big Bright Academy Hall
明秀學堂 Elegant Academic Hall
明秀學堂 Elegant Academic Hall
聰明學堂 Intelligent Academic Hall
聰明學堂 Intelligent Academic Hall
忠信學堂 Loyal Academic Hall
廣德學堂 Broad Virtuous Academic Hall

The Bamboo-Shoot Level Academic Hall
班筍學堂

The Bamboo-Shoot Level Academic Hall is represented by the eyebrows.

The ideal eyebrows are long and dense, but not too dense, with a neat, uniform appearance and eyebrow hair that grows in one direction as opposed to being scraggly or scant.

This Hall indicates whether a person is likely to enjoy good partnerships and working relationships with others. Long, elegant eyebrows that are well-defined tend to also denote a long, healthy life.

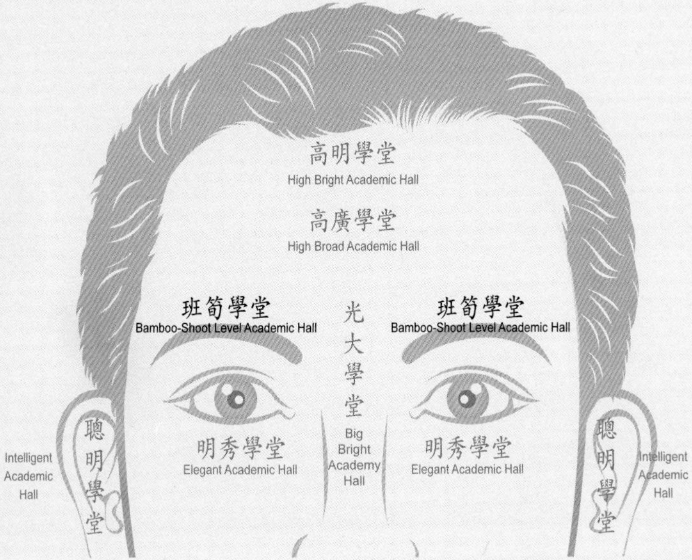

高明學堂
High Bright Academic Hall

高廣學堂
High Broad Academic Hall

班筍學堂
Bamboo-Shoot Level Academic Hall

班筍學堂
Bamboo-Shoot Level Academic Hall

光大學堂
Big Bright Academy Hall

明秀學堂
Elegant Academic Hall

明秀學堂
Elegant Academic Hall

聰明學堂
Intelligent Academic Hall

聰明學堂
Intelligent Academic Hall

宮位

About Joey Yap

Joey Yap first began learning about Chinese Metaphysics from masters in the field when he was fifteen.

Despite having graduated with a Commerce degree in Accounting, Joey never became an accountant. Instead, he began to give seminars, talks and professional Chinese Metaphysic consultations in Malaysia, Singapore, India, Australia, Canada, England, Germany and the United States, becoming a household name in the field.

By the age of twenty-six, Joey became a self-made millionaire and in 2008, he was listed in The Malaysian Tatler as the Top 300 Most Influential People in Malaysia and Prestige's Top 40 Under 40.

His practical and result-driven take on Feng Shui and BaZi sets him apart from other older, traditional masters and practitioners in the field. He shows people how the ancient teachings can be utilized for tangible REAL world benefits. The success he and his clients enjoy, thanks to his advice, is positive proof that Feng Shui and BaZi Astrology works, whether everyone believes in it or not!

Today, Joey has helped and worked with governments and the wealthiest people in Singapore, Hong Kong, China, Malaysia and Japan. His clients include multinationals, developers, tycoons and royalties. On Bloomberg, he is featured on-air as a regular guest on the subject of Feng Shui annual forecasts. He is retained by twenty-five top Malaysian property developers to help determine suitable candidates to take top management, change their space and Feng Shui mechanism, the way they make decisions, and understand the natural cosmic energies that can influence their decision-making.

Every year he conducts his 'Feng Shui and Astrology' seminar to a crowd of more than 3500 people at the Kuala Lumpur Convention Center. He also takes this annual seminar on a world tour to Frankfurt, San Francisco, New York, Las Vegas, Toronto, Sydney and Singapore.

The Joey Yap Consulting Group is the world's largest and first specialized metaphysics consultation firm. His consultancy, and professional speaking and training engagements with Microsoft, HP, Bloomberg, Citibank, HSBC and many more have seen the benefits of Classical Feng Shui and BaZi find their way into corporate environment and culture. Celebrities, property developers and other large organizations turn to Joey when they need the best.

After years of field-testing and fine-tuning his teachings, he has put together a team in the form of Joey Yap Research International. The objective of this Research Team is to scientifically track and verify the positive impact of Feng Shui and BaZi on subjects and ultimately to assist more people in achieving their life goals.

The Mastery Academy of Chinese Metaphysics which Joey founded teaches thousands of students from all around the world about Classical Feng Shui, Chinese Astrology and Face Reading. Many graduates have gone on to become successful in their own right, becoming sought after consultants, setting up their own consultancy businesses or even becoming educators, passing on Chinese Metaphysics knowledge to others.

Joey has also created the Decision Referential Technology™, offering decision reformation training on how to make better decisions in business and in personal life. He has led his team of highly trained consultants to help clients create more positive change in corporate boardrooms and increase production in their companies, helping people see their business outlook for each year so they may anticipate, plan and execute their strategies successfully.

Joey's work has been featured regularly in various popular global publications and networks like Time, Forbes, the International Herald Tribune and Bloomberg. He has also written columns for The New Straits Times, The Star and The Edge – Malaysia's leading newspapers. He has achieved bestselling author status with over sixty-five books, which have sold more than three million copies to-date.

His success is not limited to matters of Feng Shui and BaZi. Although his success is a product of them, he is also a successful entrepreneur, leading his own companies and property investment portfolio. When not teaching metaphysics or consulting around the world, Joey is a Naruto-fan, avid snowboarder and is crazy for fruits de mer.

Author's personal website :

 www.joeyyap.com

Joey Yap on Facebook:

 www.facebook.com/JoeyYapFB

MASTERY ACADEMY
OF CHINESE METAPHYSICS
Your **Preferred** Choice to the Art & Science of Classical Chinese Metaphysics Studies

Bringing **innovative** techniques and **creative** teaching methods to an ancient study.

Mastery Academy of Chinese Metaphysics was established by Joey Yap to play the role of disseminating this Eastern knowledge to the modern world with the belief that this valuable knowledge should be accessible to anyone, anywhere.

Its goal is to enrich people's lives through accurate, professional teaching and practice of Chinese Metaphysics knowledge globally. It is the first academic institution of its kind in the world to adopt the tradition of Western institutions of higher learning - where students are encourage to explore, question and challenge themselves and to respect different fields and branches of study - with the appreciation and respect of classical ideas and applications that have stood the test of time.

The art and science of Chinese Metaphysics studies – be it Feng Shui, BaZi (Astrology), Mian Xiang (Face Reading), ZeRi (Date Selection) or Yi Jing – is no longer a field shrouded with mystery and superstition. In light of new technology, fresher interpretations and innovative methods as well as modern teaching tools like the Internet, interactive learning, e-learning and distance learning, anyone from virtually any corner of the globe, who is keen to master these disciplines can do so with ease and confidence under the guidance and support of the Academy.

It has indeed proven to be a center of educational excellence for thousands of students from over thirty countries across the world; many of whom have moved on to practice classical Chinese Metaphysics professionally in their home countries.

At the Academy, we believe in enriching people's lives by empowering their destinies through the disciplines of Chinese Metaphysics. Learning is not an option - it's a way of life!

MALAYSIA
19-3, The Boulevard, Mid Valley City, 59200 Kuala Lumpur, Malaysia
Tel : +603-2284 8080 | Fax : +603-2284 1218
Email   : info@masteryacademy.com
Website : www.masteryacademy.com

Australia, Austria, Canada, China, Croatia, Cyprus, Czech Republic, Denmark, France, Germany, Greece, Hungary, India, Italy, Kazakhstan, Malaysia, Netherlands (Holland), New Zealand, Philippines, Poland, Russian Federation, Singapore, Slovenia, South Africa, Switzerland, Turkey, U.S.A., Ukraine, United Kingdom

Mastery Academy around the world

www.masteryacademy.com | +603 - 2284 8080

JOEY YAP CONSULTING GROUP

Pioneering Metaphysics - Centric Personal Coaching and Corporate Consulting

The Joey Yap Consulting Group is the world's first specialised metaphysics consultation firm. Founded in 2002 by renown international Feng Shui and BaZi consultant, author and trainer Joey Yap, the Joey Yap Consulting Group is a pioneer in the provision of metaphysics-driven coaching and consultation services for individuals and corporations.

The Group's core consultation practice areas are Feng Shui and BaZi, which are complimented by ancillary services like Date Selection, Face Reading and Yi Jing Divination. The Group's team of highly-trained professional consultants are led by Principal Consultant Joey Yap. The Joey Yap Consulting Group is the firm of choice for corporate captains, entrepreneurs, celebrities and property developers when it comes to Feng Shui and BaZi-related advisory and knowledge.

Across Industries: Our Portfolio of Clients

Our diverse portfolio of both corporate and individual clients from all around the world bears testimony to our experience and capabilities.

Joey Yap Consulting Group is the firm of choice for many of Asia's leading multi-national corporations, listed entities, conglomerates and top-tier property developers when it comes to Feng Shui and corporate BaZi.

Our services also engaged by professionals, prominent business personalities, celebrities, high-profile politicians and people from all walks of life.

JOEY YAP CONSULTING GROUP

Name (Mr./Mrs./Ms.):_____

Contact Details

Tel:_____ Fax:_____

Mobile :_____

E-mail:_____

What Type of Consultation Are You Interested In?
☐ Feng Shui ☐ BaZi ☐ Date Selection ☐ Corporate Events

Please tick if applicable:
☐ Are you a Property Developer looking to engage Joey Yap Consulting Group?

☐ Are you a Property Investor looking for tailor-made packages to suit your investment requirements?

Please attach your name card here.

Thank you for completing this form. Please fax it back to us at:

Malaysia & the rest of the world
Fax : +603-2284 2213   Tel : +603-2284 1213

www.joeyyap.com

Feng Shui Consultations

For Residential Properties
- Initial Land/Property Assessment
- Residential Feng Shui Consultations
- Residential Land Selection
- End-to-End Residential Consultation

For Commercial Properties
- Initial Land/Property Assessment
- Commercial Feng Shui Consultations
- Commercial Land Selection
- End-to-End Commercial Consultation

For Property Developers
- End-to-End Consultation
- Post-Consultation Advisory Services
- Panel Feng Shui Consultant

For Property Investors
- Your Personal Feng Shui Consultant
- Tailor-Made Packages

For Memorial Parks & Burial Sites
- Yin House Feng Shui

BaZi Consultations

Personal Destiny Analysis
- Personal Destiny Analysis for Individuals
- Children's BaZi Analysis
- Family BaZi Analysis

Strategic Analysis for Corporate Organizations
- Corporate BaZi Consultations
- BaZi Analysis for Human Resource Management

Entrepreneurs & Business Owners
- BaZi Analysis for Entrepreneurs

Career Pursuits
- BaZi Career Analysis

Relationships
- Marriage and Compatibility Analysis
- Partnership Analysis

For Everyone
- Annual BaZi Forecast
- Your Personal BaZi Coach

Date Selection Consultations

- **Marriage Date Selection**
- **Caesarean Birth Date Selection**
- **House-Moving Date Selection**
- **Renovation & Groundbreaking Dates**
- **Signing of Contracts**
- **Official Openings**
- **Product Launches**

Corporate Events

Many reputable organizations and instituitions have worked closely with Joey Yap Consulting Group to build a synergistic business relationship by engaging our team of consultants, led by Joey Yap, as speakers at their corporate events.

We tailor our seminars and talks to suit the anticipated or pertinent group of audience. Be it department, subsidiary, your clients or even the entire corporation, we aim to fit your requirements in delivering the intended message(s).

Tel: +603-2284 1213   Email: consultation@joeyyap.com

CHINESE METAPHYSICS REFERENCE SERIES

The Chinese Metaphysics Reference Series is a collection of reference texts, source material, and educational textbooks to be used as supplementary guides by scholars, students, researchers, teachers and practitioners of Chinese Metaphysics.

These comprehensive and structured books provide fast, easy reference to aid in the study and practice of various Chinese Metaphysics subjects including Feng Shui, BaZi, Yi Jing, Zi Wei, Liu Ren, Ze Ri, Ta Yi, Qi Men and Mian Xiang.

The Chinese Metaphysics Compendium

At over 1,000 pages, the *Chinese Metaphysics Compendium* is a unique one-volume reference book that compiles all the formulas relating to Feng Shui, BaZi (Four Pillars of Destiny), Zi Wei (Purple Star Astrology), Yi Jing (I-Ching), Qi Men (Mystical Doorways), Ze Ri (Date Selection), Mian Xiang (Face Reading) and other sources of Chinese Metaphysics.

It is presented in the form of easy-to-read tables, diagrams and reference charts, all of which are compiled into one handy book. This first-of-its-kind compendium is presented in both English and the original Chinese, so that none of the meanings and contexts of the technical terminologies are lost.

The only essential and comprehensive reference on Chinese Metaphysics, and an absolute must-have for all students, scholars, and practitioners of Chinese Metaphysics.

The Ten Thousand Year Calendar (Pocket Edition)

The Ten Thousand Year Calendar

Dong Gong Date Selection

The Date Selection Compendium

Plum Blossoms Divination Reference Book

San Yuan Dragon Gate Eight Formations Water Method

Xuan Kong Da Gua Ten Thousand Year Calendar

Bazi Hour Pillar Useful Gods - Wood

Bazi Hour Pillar Useful Gods - Fire

Bazi Hour Pillar Useful Gods - Earth

Bazi Hour Pillar Useful Gods - Metal

Bazi Hour Pillar Useful Gods - Water

Xuan Kong Da Gua Structures Reference Book

Xuan Kong Da Gua 64 Gua Transformation Analysis

Bazi Structures and Structural Useful Gods - Wood

Bazi Structures and Structural Useful Gods - Fire

Bazi Structures and Structural Useful Gods - Earth

Bazi Structures and Structural Useful Gods - Metal

Bazi Structures and Structural Useful Gods - Water

Xuan Kong Purple White Script

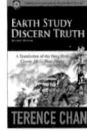
Earth Study Discern Truth Second Edition

www.masteryacademy.com | +603 - 2284 8080

Joey Yap's BaZi Profiling System

Three Levels of BaZi Profiling (English & Chinese versions)

In BaZi Profiling, there are three levels that reflect three different stages of a person's personal nature and character structure.

Level 1 – The Day Master

The Day Master in a nutshell is the BASIC YOU. The inborn personality. It is your essential character. It answers the basic question "WHO AM I". There are ten basic personality profiles – the TEN Day Masters – each with its unique set of personality traits, likes and dislikes.

Level 2 – The Structure

The Structure is your behavior and attitude – in other words, how you use your personality. It expands on the Day Master (Level 1). The structure reveals your natural tendencies in life – are you more controlling, more of a creator, supporter, thinker or connector? Each of the Ten Day Masters express themselves differently through the FIVE Structures. Why do we do the things we do? Why do we like the things we like? – The answers are in our BaZi STRUCTURE.

Level 3 – The Profile

The Profile reveals your unique abilities and skills, the masks that you consciously and unconsciously "put on" as you approach and navigate the world. Your Profile speaks of your ROLES in life. There are TEN roles – or Ten BaZi Profiles. Everyone plays a different role.

What makes you happy and what does success mean to you is different to somebody else. Your sense of achievement and sense of purpose in life is unique to your Profile. Your Profile will reveal your unique style.

The path of least resistance to your success and wealth can only be accessed once you get into your "flow." Your BaZi Profile reveals how you can get FLOW. It will show you your patterns in work, relationship and social settings. Being AWARE of these patterns is your first step to positive Life Transformation.

www.baziprofiling.com

BaZi Collections

Leading Chinese Astrology Master Trainer Joey Yap makes it easy to learn how to unlock your Destiny through your BaZi with these books. BaZi or Four Pillars of Destiny is an ancient Chinese science which enables individuals to understand their personality, hidden talents and abilities as well as their luck cycle, simply by examining the information contained within their birth data.

Understand and appreciate more about this astoundingly accurate ancient Chinese Metaphysical science with this BaZi Collection.

Feng Shui Collection

Must-Haves for Property Analysis!

For homeowners, those looking to build their own home or even investors who are looking to apply Feng Shui to their homes, these series of books provides valuable information from the classical Feng Shui therioes and applications.

In his trademark straight-to-the-point manner, Joey shares with you the Feng Shui do's and dont's when it comes to finding a property with favorable Feng Shui, which is condusive for home living.

Stories & Lessons on Feng Shui Series

All in all, this series is a delightful chronicle of Joey's articles, thoughts and vast experience - as a professional Feng Shui consultant and instructor - that have been purposely refined, edited and expanded upon to make for a light-hearted, interesting yet educational read. And with Feng Shui, BaZi, Mian Xiang and Yi Jing all thrown into this one dish, there's something for everyone.

www.masteryacademy.com | +603 - 2284 8080

Continue Your Journey with Joey Yap Books in Feng Shui

Pure Feng Shui
Pure Feng Shui is Joey Yap's debut with an international publisher, CICO Books, and is a refreshing and elegant look at the intricacies of Classical Feng Shui – now compiled in a useful manner for modern-day readers. This book is a comprehensive introduction to all the important precepts and techniques of Feng Shui practice.

Your Aquarium Here
This book is the first in Fengshuilogy Series, a series of matter-in-fact and useful Feng Shui books designed for the person who wants to do a fuss-free Feng Shui.

Xuan Kong Flying Stars
This book is an essential introductory book to the subject of Xuan Kong Fei Xing, a well-known and popular system of Feng Shui. Learn 'tricks of the trade' and 'trade secrets' to enhance and maximize Qi in your home or office.

Walking the Dragons
Compiled in one book for the first time from Joey Yap's Feng Shui Mastery Excursion Series, the book highlights China's extensive, vibrant history with astute observations on the Feng Shui of important sites and places. Learn the landform formations of Yin Houses (tombs and burial places), as well as mountains, temples, castles, and villages.

The Art of Date Selection: Personal Date Selection
With the *Art of Date Selection: Personal Date Selection*, learn simple, practical methods you can employ to select not just good dates, but personalized good dates. Whether it's a personal activity such as a marriage or professional endeavor such as launching a business, signing a contract or even acquiring assets, this book will show you how to pick the good dates and tailor them to suit the activity in question, as well as avoid the negative ones too!

www.masteryacademy.com | +603 - 2284 8080

Face Reading Collection

Discover Face Reding (English & Chinese versions)

This is a comprehensive book on all areas of Face Reading, covering some of the most important facial features, including the forehead, mouth, ears and even philtrum above your lips. This book cill help you analyse not just your Destiny but help you achieve your full potential and achieve life fulfillment.

Joey Yap's Art of Face Reading

The Art of Face Reading is Joey Yap's second effort with CICO Books, and takes a lighter, more practical approach to Face Reading. This book does not so much focus on the individual features as it does on reading the entire face. It is about identifying common personality types and characters.

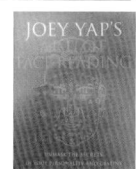

Easy Guide on Face Reading (English & Chinese versions)

The Face Reading Essentials series of books comprises 5 individual books on the key features of the face – Eyes, Eyebrows, Ears, Nose, and Mouth. Each book provides a detailed illustration and a simple yet descriptive explanation on the individual types of the features.

The books are equally useful and effective for beginners, enthusiasts, and the curious. The series is designed to enable people who are new to Face Reading to make the most of first impressions and learn to apply Face Reading skills to understand the personality and character of friends, family, co-workers, and even business associates.

Annual Releases
2011 Annual Outlook & Tong Shu

| Chinese Astrology for 2011 | Feng Shui for 2011 | Tong Shu Desktop Calendar 2011 | Professional Tong Shu Diary 2011 | Tong Shu Monthly Planner 2011 | Weekly Tong Shu Diary 2011 |

www.masteryacademy.com | +603 - 2284 8080

Educational Tools and Software

Xuan Kong Flying Stars Feng Shui Software
The Essential Application for Enthusiasts and Professionals

The Xuan Kong Flying Stars Feng Shui Software will assist you in the practice of Xuan Kong Feng Shui with minimum fuss and maximum effectiveness. Superimpose the Flying Stars charts over your house plans (or those of your clients) to clearly demarcate the 9 Palaces. Use it to help you create fast and sophisticated chart drawings and presentations, as well as to assist professional practitioners in the report-writing process before presenting the final reports for your clients. Students can use it to practice their Xuan Kong Feng Shui skills and knowledge, and it can even be used by designers and architects!

BaZi Ming Pan Software Version 2.0
Professional Four Pillars Calculator for Destiny Analysis

The BaZi Ming Pan Version 2.0 Professional Four Pillars Calculator for Destiny Analysis is the most technically advanced software of its kind in the world today. It allows even those without any knowledge of BaZi to generate their own BaZi Charts, and provides virtually every detail required to undertake a comprehensive Destiny Analysis.

This Professional Four Pillars Calculator allows you to even undertake a day-to-day analysis of your Destiny. What's more, all BaZi Charts generated by this software are fully printable and configurable! Designed for both enthusiasts and professional practitioners, this state-of-the-art software blends details with simplicity, and is capable of generating 4 different types of BaZi charts: **BaZi Professional Charts, BaZi Annual Analysis Charts, BaZi Pillar Analysis Charts and BaZi Family Relationship Charts.**

Joey Yap Feng Shui Template Set

Directions are the cornerstone of any successful Feng Shui audit or application. The **Joey Yap Feng Shui Template Set** is a set of three templates to simplify the process of taking directions and determining locations and positions, whether it's for a building, a house, or an open area such as a plot of land, all with just a floor plan or area map.

The Set comprises 3 basic templates: The Basic Feng Shui Template, 8 Mansions Feng Shui Template, and the Flying Stars Feng Shui Template.

Mini Feng Shui Compass

The Mini Feng Shui Compass is a self-aligning compass that is not only light at 100gms but also built sturdily to ensure it will be convenient to use anywhere. The rings on the Mini Feng Shui Compass are bi-lingual and incorporate the 24 Mountain Rings that is used in your traditional Luo Pan.

The comprehensive booklet included will guide you in applying the 24 Mountain Directions on your Mini Feng Shui Compass effectively and the 8 Mansions Feng Shui to locate the most auspicious locations within your home, office and surroundings. You can also use the Mini Feng Shui Compass when measuring the direction of your property for the purpose of applying Flying Stars Feng Shui.

---

www.masteryacademy.com | +603 - 2284 8080

Educational Tools and Software

Xuan Kong Vol.1
An Advanced Feng Shui Home Study Course

Learn the Xuan Kong Flying Star Feng Shui system in just 20 lessons! Joey Yap's specialised notes and course work have been written to enable distance learning without compromising on the breadth or quality of the syllabus. Learn at your own pace with the same material students in a live class would use. The most comprehensive distance learning course on Xuan Kong Flying Star Feng Shui in the market. Xuan Kong Flying Star Vol.1 comes complete with a special binder for all your course notes.

Feng Shui for Period 8 - (DVD)

Don't miss the Feng Shui Event of the next 20 years! Catch Joey Yap LIVE and find out just what Period 8 is all about. This DVD boxed set zips you through the fundamentals of Feng Shui and the impact of this important change in the Feng Shui calendar. Joey's entertaining, conversational style walks you through the key changes that Period 8 will bring and how to tap into Wealth Qi and Good Feng Shui for the next 20 years.

Xuan Kong Flying Stars Beginners Workshop - (DVD)

Take a front row seat in Joey Yap's Xuan Kong Flying Stars workshop with this unique LIVE RECORDING of Joey Yap's Xuan Kong Flying Stars Feng Shui workshop, attended by over 500 people. This DVD program provides an effective and quick introduction of Xuan Kong Feng Shui essentials for those who are just starting out in their study of classical Feng Shui. Learn to plot your own Flying Star chart in just 3 hours. Learn 'trade secret' methods, remedies and cures for Flying Stars Feng Shui. This boxed set contains 3 DVDs and 1 workbook with notes and charts for reference.

BaZi Four Pillars of Destiny Beginners Workshop - (DVD)

Ever wondered what Destiny has in store for you? Or curious to know how you can learn more about your personality and inner talents? BaZi or Four Pillars of Destiny is an ancient Chinese science that enables us to understand a person's hidden talent, inner potential, personality, health and wealth luck from just their birth data. This specially compiled DVD set of Joey Yap's BaZi Beginners Workshop provides a thorough and comprehensive introduction to BaZi. Learn how to read your own chart and understand your own luck cycle. This boxed set contains 3 DVDs and 1 workbook with notes and reference charts.

---

www.masteryacademy.com | +603 - 2284 8080

DVD Series

Joey Yap's Face Reading Revealed DVD Series

Mian Xiang, the Chinese art of Face Reading, is an ancient form of physiognomy and entails the use of the face and facial characteristics to evaluate key aspects of a person's life, luck and destiny. In his Face Reading DVDs series, Joey Yap shows you how the facial features reveal a wealth of information about a person's luck, destiny and personality.

Mian Xiang also tell us the talents, quirks and personality of an individual. Do you know that just by looking at a person's face, you can ascertain his or her health, wealth, relationships and career? Let Joey Yap show you how the 12 Palaces can be utilised to reveal a person's inner talents, characteristics and much more.

Feng Shui for Homebuyers DVD Series

In these DVDs, you will also learn how to identify properties with good Feng Shui features that will help you promote a fulfilling life and achieve your full potential. Discover how to avoid properties with negative Feng Shui that can bring about detrimental effects to your health, wealth and relationships.

Joey will also elaborate on how to fix the various aspects of your home that may have an impact on the Feng Shui of your property and give pointers on how to tap into the positive energies to support your goals.

Discover Feng Shui with Joey Yap: Set of 4 DVDs
Informative and entertaining, classical Feng Shui comes alive in *Discover Feng Shui with Joey Yap!*

You have the questions. Now let Joey personally answer them in this 4-set DVD compilation! Learn how to ensure the viability of your residence or workplace, Feng Shui-wise, without having to convert it into a Chinese antiques' shop. Classical Feng Shui is about harnessing the natural power of your environment to improve quality of life. It's a systematic and subtle metaphysical science.

Walking the Dragons with Joey Yap (The TV Series)

This DVD set features eight episodes, covering various landform Feng Shui analyses and applications from Joey Yap as he and his co-hosts travel through China. It includes case studies of both modern and historical sites with a focus on Yin House (burial places) Feng Shui and the tombs of the Qing Dynasty emperors.

The series was partly filmed on-location in mainland China, and the state of Selangor, Malaysia.

www.masteryacademy.com | +603 - 2284 8080

Home Study Courses

Gain Valuable Knowledge from the Comfort of Your Home

Now, armed with your trusty computer or laptop and Internet access, knowledge of Chinese Metaphysics is just a click away!

3 easy steps to activate your Home Study Course:

Step 1:
Go to the URL as indicated on the Activation Card, and key in your Activation Code

Step 2:
At the Registration page, fill in the details accordingly to enable us to generate your Student Identification (Student ID).

Step 3:
Upon successful registration, you may begin your lessons immediately.

Joey Yap's Feng Shui Mastery HomeStudy Course

Module 1: **Empowering Your Home**
Module 2: **Master Practitioner Program**

Learn how easy it is to harness the power of the environment to promote health, wealth and prosperity in your life. The knowledge and applications of Feng Shui will no more be a mystery but a valuable tool you can master on your own.

Joey Yap's BaZi Mastery HomeStudy Course

Module 1: **Mapping Your Life**
Module 2: **Mastering Your Future**

Discover your path of least resistance to success with insights about your personality and capabilities, and what strengths you can tap on to maximize your potential for success and happiness by mastering BaZi (Chinese Astrology). This course will teach you all the essentials you need to interpret a BaZi chart and more.

Joey Yap's Mian Xiang Mastery HomeStudy Course

Module 1: **Face Reading**
Module 2: **Advanced Face Reading**

A face can reveal so much about a person. Now, you can learn the art and science of Mian Xiang (Chinese Face Reading) to understand a person's character based on his or her facial features with ease and confidence.

www.masteryacademy.com | +603 - 2284 8080

Feng Shui Mastery™
LIVE COURSES (MODULES ONE TO FOUR)

The Feng Shui Mastery™ comprises Feng Shui Mastery Modules 1, 2, 3 and 4. It starts off with a foundation program up to the advanced practitioner level. It is a thorough, comprehensive program that covers important theories from various classical Feng Shui systems including Ba Zhai, San Yuan, San He, and Xuan Kong.

Module One: Beginners Course **Module Two:** Practitioners Course **Module Three:** Advanced Practitioners Course **Module Four:** Master Course

BaZi Mastery™
LIVE COURSES (MODULES ONE TO FOUR)

The BaZi Mastery™ consists of BaZi Mastery Modules 1, 2, 3 and 4. In Modules 1 and 2, students will receive a thorough introduction to BaZi, along with an intensive understanding of BaZi principles and the requisite skills to practice it with accuracy and precision. This will prepare them, and serious Feng Shui practitioners, for a more advanced levels and fine-tune their application skills in Modules 3 and 4.

Module One: Intensive Foundation Course **Module Two:** Practitioners Course **Module Three:** Advanced Practitioners Course **Module Four:** Master Course in BaZi

Xuan Kong Mastery™
LIVE COURSES (MODULES ONE TO THREE)
* Advanced Courses For Master Practitioners

The Xuan Kong Mastery™ comprises Xuan Kong Mastery Modules 1, 2A, 2B and 3. It is a sophisticated branch of Feng Shui replete with many techniques and formulae, enabling practitioners to evaluate Feng Shui on a more thorough and in-depth basis. The study of Xuan Kong encompasses numerology, symbology and science of the Ba Gua along with the mathematics of time.

Module One: Advanced Foundation Course **Module Two A:** Advanced Xuan Kong Methodologies **Module Two B:** Purple White **Module Three:** Advanced Xuan Kong Da Gua

www.masteryacademy.com | +603 - 2284 8080

Mian Xiang Mastery™
LIVE COURSES (MODULES ONE AND TWO)

The Mian Xiang Mastery™ comprises of Mian Xiang Mastery Modules 1 and 2 to allow students to learn this ancient art in a thorough, detailed manner. Each module has a carefully-developed syllabus that allows students to get acquainted with the fundamentals of Mian Xiang before moving on to the more intricate theories and principles that will enable them to practice Mian Xiang with greater depth and complexity.

Module One:
Basic Face Reading

Module Two:
Practical Face Reading

Yi Jing Mastery™
LIVE COURSES (MODULES ONE AND TWO)

The Yi Jing Mastery™ comprises Modules 1 and 2. Both Modules aim to give casual and serious Yi Jing enthusiasts a serious insight into one of the most important philosophical treatises in ancient Chinese thought. Yi Jing uses sophisticated formulas and calculations to derive the answers to questions we pose. It is a science of divination, and in our classes there is a heavy emphasis on the scientific aspect of it. It bears no religious or superstitious affiliation.

Module One:
Traditional Yi Jing

Module Two:
Plum Blossom Numerology

Ze Ri Mastery™
LIVE COURSES (MODULES ONE AND TWO)

The ZeRi Mastery™ consists of ZeRi Mastery Modules 1 and 2. This program provides students with a thorough introduction to the art of Date Selection both for Personal and Feng Shui purposes. Our ZeRi Mastery™ aims to provide a thorough and comprehensive program on the art of Date Selection, covering everything from Personal and Feng Shui Date Selection to Xuan Kong Da Gua Date Selection.

Module One:
Personal and Feng Shui Date Selection

Module Two:
Xuan Kong Da Gua Date Selection